D0468399

Purchased from
Multnomah County Library
Title Wave Used Bookstore
216 NE Knott St, Portland, OR
503-988-5021

WILLIAMS-SONOMA

NEW FLAVORS FOR
salads

RECIPES
Dina Cheney

PHOTOGRAPHS
Kate Sears

Oxmoor
House®

spring

summer

fall

winter

introducing new flavors

A classic salad is classic for a reason: It's a delicious composition of tastes and textures that has an enduring appeal. Sometimes, though, shaking it up a bit with international flavor accents and impeccably fresh local produce yields a dish that both surprises and delights the palate in a way that a classic simply does not. When seasonings from faraway and locally grown ingredients unite, traditional dishes like Caesar salad or Italian panzanella take on enticing new profiles.

Salads are uniquely elemental, so using highest quality, peak-season produce is key to building character—juicy summer peaches bring so much more personality to a salad than the sad, weak samples flown in from from distant lands in the winter. Along with quality that can be tasted, we have variety to explore in our salad making—Vidalia onions, fava beans, poblano chiles, Asian pears. With such a breadth of local, seasonal, and organic produce more available than ever, there's no reason to settle for anything less than fresh, ripe, and full flavored.

At our fingertips, we also have global ingredients such as Spanish smoked paprika, Peruvian quinoa, and imported cheeses to impart bold new tastes, richness, and complexity. Invite these elements into your salads: You'll be broadening your ingredient base and achieving a lively assortment of flavor combinations.

You'll find plenty of inspiration in these pages: Forty-four alluring, thoughtfully crafted, colorful salads, organized by the seasons when their components are freshest and most flavorful. They are based, sometimes loosely, on familiar favorites but all will taste like inspired new classics that will supplement your first-course, main-dish, and side-dish salad repertory.

freshness as an ingredient

Fruits and vegetables, not cooking techniques, are the stars of salads. Without browning, braising, or sautéeing to hide behind, there's no way to disguise limp, sub par lettuce or spongy, second-rate cucumbers. Instead, the raw ingredients must be brimming with freshness and bursting with character.

local The next best thing to growing your own fruits, vegetables, and herbs is shopping at farmers' markets, farm stands, and grocery stores that source just-picked, local produce. With such top-notch ingredients, there's little need to embellish them, hence their natural place in salads. Locally grown produce barely travels, meaning that it arrives at the market fresher and, consequently, it packs in more flavor and aroma than produce that has been shipped in from afar. As an added bonus, by buying local, you're helping the community and local farmers that need your support.

seasonal By using fruits and vegetables that are harvested at the height of their season, you're experiencing them at their peak. What could be sweeter and more perfumed than English peas in the pods in the springtime or sun-ripened tomatoes in the summer? The most flavorful salads keep pace with nature and feature what is best at the moment, so for inspiration, look no further than what is in season.

organic Organic produce has neither been sprayed with pesticides nor exposed to life-extending preservatives. As a result, it's naturally fresher, and thus more delicious. Though it may cost a bit more and have a less-perfect appearance than the products of conventional farming, organic produce is produce at its best, with an integrity of flavor and appearance.

being bold

High-impact seasonings, surprising combinations of ingredients, and flavor-focused techniques are the keys to creating wonderful salads. With these in mind, we're able to infuse salads—including classics and old favorites—with bold new tastes, aromas, colors, and textures.

global seasonings Spicy Sriracha sauce, toasty Marcona almonds, pungent fish sauce, tangy pomegranate molasses—although rapidly becoming staples of American cooking, joining extra-virgin olive oil and balsamic vinegar on the pantry shelf, high-impact international ingredients such as these were once considered exotic. But thanks to gourmet and specialty stores, cheese shops, and even well-stocked supermarkets, we have a global pantry within our reach.

unexpected pairings Forging unusual juxtapositions is a way to bring wonderful elements of surprise to salads. Potato salad gets peppery flavor and satisfying crunch from diced radishes; a watermelon salad pairs the fruit's sweetness with the salty tang of ricotta salata cheese; a carrot and raisin salad becomes earthier and more robust by the addition of grated parsnips. The result of such matches are dishes that engage the palate with every bite.

flavorful cooking methods While most of the salads in this book highlight fruits and vegetables in the raw, a handful of recipes incorporate simple cooking methods that amplify tastes. Toasting draws out the character of spices and makes them smell and taste more intense. Roasting fruits and vegetables concentrates their flavors and caramelizes their natural sugars for added depth. Grilling infuses fruits, vegetables, meats, and seafood with seductive hints of smokiness.

flavors in layers

The thoughtful layering of flavors and textures is of great importance in a salad because without it, the salad runs the risk of being extremely dull or unnecessarily chaotic. The components must work well together, and the dressing should provide a brightness that unites them without being overwhelming.

complementary and contrasting flavors Many dishes feature elements that complement, or build on, each other, such as walnut oil extending the taste of toasted walnuts that coat rounds of fresh goat cheese. Similarly, earthy lentils find a perfect match in the vegetal quality of kale and the smokiness of bacon. Other salads feature contrasting tastes: A tangy berry dressing balances the richness of seared duck breast. Hot, sour, salty, and sweet incorporated into a Southeast Asian–inspired pomelo salad create a complex flavor profile.

texture, temperature, and color Different textures, temperatures, and colors integrated into a single salad have a dramatic effect: They make you stop and take notice. In these pages, you'll find recipes that carefully consider these qualities. Creamy-textured yellow mangoes are mixed with crisp, pale-white jicama and tossed with a green-speckled cilantro dressing. A sweet-sour salad of edamame and cucumbers tastes even more refreshing because it is served chilled. A warm vinaigrette over spinach and a poached egg is richly comforting and satisfying.

Think of these recipes as delicious, inspired ways to enjoy seasonal fruits and vegetables, ways to capture their goodness and bring them to the dinner table. With global ingredients, unexpected pairings, and flavor-boosting cooking methods, these recipes transform everyday salads into truly exceptional dishes.

spring

asparagus with lemon and shaved parmigiano-reggiano

pencil-thin asparagus,
3½ pounds

lemon, 1 large

**sea salt and freshly ground
pepper**

fruity extra-virgin olive oil,
2 tablespoons

**parmigiano-reggiano
cheese,** ⅓ pound

MAKES 6 SERVINGS

Bring a large saucepan two-thirds full of water to a boil over high heat. Fill a large bowl two-thirds full with ice water.

Trim off the tough end of each asparagus spear and cut the spears into 1½-inch lengths. Finely grate 1 tablespoon zest from the lemon and then squeeze 1 tablespoon juice.

Add 1 tablespoon salt and the asparagus pieces to the boiling water and cook until the asparagus is tender-crisp and bright green, about 2½ minutes. Drain and then immediately transfer the asparagus to the ice water. Let stand until cool, about 2 minutes, then drain again. Transfer the asparagus pieces to a serving platter.

In a small nonreactive bowl, whisk together the lemon zest and juice, ¼ teaspoon salt, and ¼ teaspoon pepper. Slowly whisk in the olive oil until well blended to make a dressing. Taste and adjust the seasonings. Drizzle the dressing evenly over the asparagus. Using a vegetable peeler, shave the cheese over the asparagus and serve right away.

In this simple first course, salty, nutty tasting Parmigiano-Reggiano provides a suitably bold contrast to the natural acidity of lemon and the grassiness of asparagus. Extra-virgin olive oil, preferably a fruity one, nicely binds together all of the elements.

watercress and duck salad with gingered strawberry dressing

This springtime salad features the classic pairing of fruit with crisp-skinned duck. Crystallized ginger lends sweetness and a piquant, slightly citrusy flavor to a strawberry dressing that balances the duck's richness. Peppery watercress complements the ginger's pleasing spiciness.

Preheat the oven to 400°F. Using a paring knife, hull the strawberries (page 145). Add 4 or 5 of the berries to a blender. Cut the remaining berries lengthwise into quarters and set aside. Add the ginger, lemon juice, sugar, and a pinch each of salt and pepper to the blender with the whole berries and process until smooth. Pour through a fine-mesh sieve into a small bowl. Slowly whisk in 1 tablespoon of the walnut oil until well blended to make a dressing. Taste and adjust the seasonings and set aside.

Using a sharp, thin-bladed knife, score the skin of each duck breast half in a ½-inch crosshatch pattern, being careful not to cut into the meat. Season each duck breast on both sides with salt and pepper.

Warm a large, heavy ovenproof sauté pan over medium-low heat for 2 minutes. Add the duck breasts, skin side down, and cook until the skin is crisp and medium brown, about 5 minutes. Remove the duck from the pan, pour off and discard all but 2 tablespoons of the fat, and return the duck, skin side up, to the pan. Place the pan in the oven and cook until an instant-read thermometer inserted into the center of each breast registers 130°F for medium-rare, 10–12 minutes, or until cooked to your liking. Transfer the duck to a cutting board, tent with aluminum foil, and let rest for 5 minutes.

Meanwhile, in a small bowl, stir together the pecans and a pinch of salt. In a large bowl, combine the watercress and the quartered strawberries, drizzle with the remaining 3 tablespoons walnut oil, and season with a scant ¼ teaspoon each of salt and pepper. Toss well. Divide the greens and berries evenly among individual plates.

Thinly slice the duck breasts on the diagonal. Fan an equal amount of duck slices on top of the greens on each plate. Drizzle each serving with the dressing, dividing it evenly, and sprinkle with the pecans. Serve right away.

large strawberries, 2 pints (1 pound total weight)

crystallized ginger, 1½ teaspoons minced

fresh lemon juice, 1½ teaspoons

sugar, 1 teaspoon

sea salt and freshly ground pepper

walnut oil, 4 tablespoons

boneless muscovy duck breast halves, 2 (about ¾ pound each)

pecans, ¾ cup, toasted (page 145) and coarsely chopped

watercress, 2 small bunches, stems removed

MAKES 4 SERVINGS

Coarsely cracked black peppercorns add drama and heat to silky tuna steaks that are quickly seared as if they were cuts of beef. Arugula echoes the black pepper's spiciness, while wispy slices of anise-like fennel lend a contrasting sweetness and subtle crunch.

arugula and fennel salad with black pepper—crusted tuna

balsamic vinegar, ¼ cup

shallot, 1 large, minced

dijon mustard, 2 teaspoons

sugar, ½ teaspoon

sea salt

extra-virgin olive oil, 10 tablespoons

vidalia onions, 2 small, thinly sliced

black peppercorns, 2 tablespoons

tuna steaks, 6 (2 pounds total weight), each about 1 inch thick

arugula leaves, 8 cups, stems removed

fennel bulb, 1 large, cored and thinly sliced

green onions, 2, green tops thinly sliced

MAKES 6 SERVINGS

In a small nonreactive bowl, whisk together the vinegar, shallot, mustard, sugar, and ¼ teaspoon salt until the sugar dissolves. Slowly whisk in 7 tablespoons of the olive oil until well blended to make a vinaigrette. Taste and adjust the seasonings and set aside.

In a large nonstick frying pan over medium heat, warm 2 tablespoons of the olive oil. Add the sliced onions and 1 teaspoon salt and sauté until softened and browned, 10–12 minutes. Transfer to a plate and set aside. Wipe the pan clean and set aside.

Place the peppercorns in a resealable plastic bag and seal closed. Using a mallet or the bottom of a small, heavy pan, coarsely crack the peppercorns. Season each tuna steak on both sides with a little salt. Then, dividing them evenly, press the cracked peppercorns into one side of each tuna steak.

Return the frying pan to medium-high heat and add the remaining 1 tablespoon olive oil. When the oil is hot but not smoking, add the tuna, peppered side down. Sear, turning once, until lightly golden on the outside and still dark pink in the center, or rare, about 2 minutes on each side, or until cooked to your liking. Transfer to a platter, tent with aluminum foil, and let rest for 5 minutes.

In a large bowl, toss together the arugula, fennel, and ¼ teaspoon salt. Whisk the vinaigrette to recombine, then drizzle about half of it over the arugula mixture and toss well. Taste and adjust the seasonings. Divide the dressed arugula mixture evenly among individual plates. Spoon the sautéed onions over the top, dividing them evenly. Thinly slice each tuna steak and arrange on top of the onions. Drizzle each salad with some of the remaining vinaigrette and sprinkle with the green onion tops. Serve right away.

Behind the boldness of black peppercorns are nuances of wine, tobacco, and fruit. Here, cracked-peppercorn crusts add dimension to mild-tasting tuna steaks. Bitter arugula, crunchy fennel, sweet caramelized onions, and an assertively flavored vinaigrette supply the supporting elements in this salad of high-contrast tastes and textures.

jicama-mango salad with cilantro dressing

Pungent, slightly lemony cilantro adds complexity and color to this refreshing salad with tropical Latin flavors. Crisp jicama and sweet mango are enlivened by the honeyed, slightly tart vinaigrette and the subtle heat of chili powder.

In a small bowl, soak the onion in cold water to cover for 15 minutes.

In a food processor, combine the cilantro, olive oil, lime juice, orange juice, honey, the ¼ teaspoon chili powder, a scant ½ teaspoon salt, and a few grinds of pepper and process until a smooth dressing forms, about 15 seconds. Taste and adjust the seasonings.

Peel the mangoes and then cut the flesh into ½-inch dice (page 145). You should have about 6 cups diced mango. Peel the jicama and cut the flesh into ½-inch dice. You should have about 4 cups diced jicama.

Drain the onion in a fine-mesh sieve and transfer to a bowl. Add the mango, jicama, ½ teaspoon salt, and ¼ teaspoon pepper. Drizzle with the dressing and toss well. Taste and adjust the seasonings.

Divide the salad evenly among chilled individual plates and garnish each serving with a light dusting of chili powder. Serve right away.

red onion, ½ cup minced

fresh cilantro,
6 tablespoons chopped

extra-virgin olive oil,
¼ cup plus 2 teaspoons

fresh lime juice,
3 tablespoons

fresh orange juice,
3 tablespoons

honey, 4 teaspoons

chili powder, ¼ teaspoon,
plus chili powder for
garnish

**sea salt and freshly ground
pepper**

mangoes, 5 (about
3½ pounds total weight)

jicama, 1 small (about
1 pound)

MAKES 6–8 SERVINGS

Cloaked with walnuts, goat cheese rounds find a buttery complement to their creaminess. Quickly baked, their warmth intensifies the onion-like flavor of a shallot-studded vinaigrette and the aroma of herbs tossed with tender greens.

spring herb salad with walnut-crusted goat cheese

champagne vinegar,
6 tablespoons

shallots, 2, minced

honey, 1 tablespoon

**sea salt and freshly ground
pepper**

walnut oil, ½ cup plus
2 tablespoons

walnuts, 3 cups, toasted
(page 145) and finely
chopped

fresh goat cheese, 2 logs
(9 ounces each)

extra-virgin olive oil, ¼ cup

**mâche, baby arugula, baby
spinach, or a combination,**
7 cups

fresh dill, 1 cup coarsely
chopped

**fresh flat-leaf parsley
leaves, 1 cup** coarsely
chopped

fresh chives, 1 cup finely
chopped

MAKES 6 SERVINGS

Preheat the oven to 350°F.

In a small nonreactive bowl, whisk together the vinegar, shallots, honey, 2 pinches of salt, and several grinds of pepper. Slowly whisk in the walnut oil until well blended to make a vinaigrette. Taste and adjust the seasonings.

In a bowl, stir together the chopped walnuts and ¼ teaspoon salt. Season each goat cheese log with salt and pepper. Using a thin-bladed knife, cut each log crosswise into 6 equal slices. Working with a few at a time, coat the slices on all sides with the walnuts, pressing gently so that the nuts adhere. Transfer the coated goat cheese rounds to a rimmed baking sheet and drizzle them lightly with the olive oil. Bake until warm, about 5 minutes.

Meanwhile, in a large bowl, toss together the mâche, dill, parsley, chives, 2 pinches of salt, and several grinds of pepper. Whisk the vinaigrette to recombine, then drizzle about one-third of it over the greens and toss well. Taste and adjust the seasonings. Divide the dressed greens evenly among individual plates. Top each serving with 2 warm goat cheese rounds, and then drizzle 2 teaspoons vinaigrette over the cheese on each serving (reserve the remaining vinaigrette for another use). Serve right away.

Walnut oil adds rich nuttiness to this salad, a quality echoed by the chopped walnuts that coat the goat cheese. Honey tempers the acidity of the Champagne vinegar in the dressing, while a trio of aromatic herbs brings vibrant flavor and color.

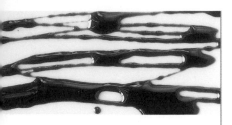

baby artichokes with garlic oil, balsamic syrup, and pine nuts

Cooking balsamic vinegar concentrates its flavor, yielding an intense sweet-tart syrup, the ultimate condiment for spring's baby artichokes. The garlic oil in the dressing adds a savory character and toasted pine nuts bring a soft crunch with woodsy, resinous hints.

In a small bowl, stir together the garlic slices and olive oil. Cover and let stand at room temperature for 1 hour.

Fill a large bowl two-thirds full with cold water. Halve the lemons. Squeeze the juice from one half into the water, and then drop in the lemon half. Juice the remaining halves to measure ¼ cup, set the juice aside, and drop the halves into the water. Working with 1 artichoke at a time, snap off the dark green outer leaves until you reach the pale green center. Cut the stem flush with the bottom and cut about ½ inch from the top. Cut the artichoke in half lengthwise and immediately add the halves to the lemon water. Repeat with the remaining artichokes.

In a large pot fitted with a steamer basket, bring 1–2 inches of water to a boil over high heat. Drain the artichokes and arrange in a single layer in the steamer basket. Cover, reduce the heat to medium, and steam until the artichokes are tender when pierced with a fork, 12–14 minutes.

Meanwhile, pour the garlic-oil mixture through a sieve into a small bowl. In another small nonreactive bowl, whisk together the reserved lemon juice, parsley, sugar, ¼ teaspoon salt, and several grinds of pepper until the sugar dissolves. Slowly whisk in the garlic oil until well blended to make a dressing. Taste and adjust the seasonings.

When the artichokes are ready, transfer them to a bowl. Whisk the dressing to recombine, then immediately add it, along with the balsamic syrup and a large pinch of salt, to the warm artichokes. Toss well. Transfer the dressed artichokes to a platter or serving bowl. In a small bowl, stir together the pine nuts and a scant ¼ teaspoon salt and sprinkle over the artichokes. Top with the cheese, if using, and serve right away.

garlic, 3 large cloves, thinly sliced

extra-virgin olive oil, ¼ cup plus 3 tablespoons

lemons, 2 large

baby artichokes, 4 pounds (about 32)

fresh flat-leaf parsley or mint, 1 tablespoon coarsely chopped

sugar, 1 teaspoon

sea salt and freshly ground pepper

balsamic syrup (page 144), 2½ tablespoons

pine nuts, ½ cup, toasted (page 145)

parmigiano-reggiano cheese, 2 ounces, shaved (optional)

MAKES 4–6 SERVINGS

israeli couscous with fava beans and olives

chicken broth, 3 cups

fresh lemon juice, ½ cup

sea salt

extra-virgin olive oil,
4 tablespoons

israeli couscous, 2⅓ cups
(¾ pound)

fava beans in their pods,
2½ pounds, shelled

carrots, 4, peeled and cut
into small dice

fresh flat-leaf parsley,
⅔ cup coarsely chopped

oil-cured black olives,
24, pitted and coarsely
chopped

feta cheese, 5 ounces,
crumbled

MAKES 6 SERVINGS

In a small nonreactive saucepan, combine the broth, lemon juice, and ½ teaspoon salt and bring to a boil over high heat. Meanwhile, in a saucepan over medium heat, warm 2 tablespoons of the olive oil. Add the couscous and cook, stirring occasionally, until light golden brown, about 4 minutes. Pour the hot broth mixture over the couscous, raise the heat to high, and bring to a boil. Cover immediately, reduce the heat to medium-low, and simmer until all of the liquid has been absorbed, about 15 minutes. Drizzle the remaining 2 tablespoons olive oil into the couscous, stir to mix, and transfer to a large bowl. Let cool to room temperature.

While the couscous cools, fill the saucepan you used to cook the couscous three-fourths full with water and bring to a boil over high heat. Fill a bowl two thirds full with ice water. Add 1 tablespoon salt and the fava beans to the boiling water and cook just until tender, about 2 minutes. Use a slotted spoon to remove the beans from the pan and immediately transfer them to the ice water. Let stand until cool, then lift out the beans with the slotted spoon. Add the carrots to the boiling salted water and cook until tender-crisp, about 2 minutes. Drain in a colander, then immediately transfer the carrots to the ice water. Let stand until cool, then drain again.

Remove the tough outer skin from each fava bean by pinching the end opposite where the bean was attached to the pod. You should have about 1¼ cups skinned beans.

Add the fava beans, carrots, parsley, olives, and cheese to the bowl with the couscous and toss well. Taste and adjust the seasonings. Transfer to a serving bowl and serve right away.

Sharp and salty feta cheese adds impact to this salad of mostly mellow flavors. It plays off the butteriness of the fava beans, the sweetness of the carrots, and the wheaty flavor of large-grained Israeli couscous.

Roasting has a surprising effect on strawberries: They become succulent and more intense in flavor. The berries' sweetness is balanced by shreds of piquant Pecorino cheese in a redefinition of the classic spinach and strawberry salad.

baby spinach salad with roasted strawberries

large strawberries, 2 pints
(1 pound total weight)

extra-virgin olive oil,
8 tablespoons

sugar, 1 tablespoon, plus
2 teaspoons

**sea salt and freshly ground
pepper**

red wine vinegar,
6 tablespoons

fresh orange juice, ¼ cup

fresh tarragon leaves,
4 teaspoons finely chopped

blanched whole almonds,
1 cup, toasted (page 145)

baby spinach, 9 cups

pecorino romano cheese,
5 ounces, shredded

MAKES 6 SERVINGS

Preheat the oven to 400°F.

Using a paring knife, hull the strawberries (page 145) and cut them in half lengthwise. Spread the berries on a rimmed baking sheet. Drizzle with 2 tablespoons of the olive oil and sprinkle with the 2 teaspoons sugar, ¼ teaspoon salt, and several grinds of pepper. Toss to coat the berries evenly, then spread them out again. Roast until softened, about 10 minutes. Let cool to room temperature.

In a small nonreactive bowl, whisk together the vinegar, orange juice, tarragon, the 1 tablespoon sugar, ¾ teaspoon salt, and several grinds of pepper until the sugar dissolves. Slowly whisk in the remaining 6 tablespoons olive oil until well blended to make a vinaigrette. Taste and adjust the seasonings.

In a small bowl, stir together the almonds and ¼ teaspoon salt. In a large bowl, combine the spinach, ¼ teaspoon salt, and several grinds of pepper. Whisk the vinaigrette to recombine, drizzle about one-third of it over the spinach, and toss well (reserve the remaining vinaigrette for another use). Taste and adjust the seasonings. Divide the dressed spinach evenly among individual plates, top each serving with an equal amount of the roasted strawberries, and sprinkle with the almonds and cheese. Serve right away.

The flavor of this salad sparkles with the bright acidity of red wine vinegar, its tartness tempered by the sweetness of fresh orange juice. Roasting strawberries with a bit of sugar intensifies their fruitiness and softens their texture, creating a nice counterpoint to the salty cheese and crunchy toasted almonds.

marinated edamame, cucumber, and red bell pepper salad

Toasted sesame seeds and sesame oil lend a nutty, earthy flavor and just a touch of bitterness to this colorful salad. In it, a sweet-sour-salty dressing inspired by Asian pickled vegetables melds with the mild taste of edamame, the coolness of cucumbers, and the satisfying crunch of red bell peppers.

In a nonreactive bowl, whisk together the vinegar, tamari, sugar, 1½ teaspoons salt, and a few grinds of pepper until the sugar dissolves. Slowly whisk in the canola and sesame oils until well blended to make a dressing. Taste and adjust the seasonings.

Pat the edamame dry with paper towels and place in a large nonreactive bowl. Cut the cucumbers into ½-inch dice and add to the bowl with the edamame. Seed the bell peppers, trim away the ribs, cut the flesh into ½-inch dice, and add to the bowl.

Whisk the dressing to recombine, then drizzle it over the vegetable mixture, sprinkle with the sesame seeds, and toss well. Cover and refrigerate for at least 1 hour or up to 1 day to blend the flavors.

When ready to serve, drain the salad and discard the dressing. Transfer to a serving bowl and serve right away.

rice vinegar, ½ cup

reduced-sodium tamari, 4 teaspoons

sugar, 5 tablespoons

sea salt and freshly ground pepper

canola oil, ⅓ cup

sesame oil, 2 teaspoons

frozen shelled edamame, 1 bag (1 pound), thawed

english cucumbers, 1½

red bell peppers, 2

sesame seeds, 3 tablespoons, toasted (page 145)

MAKES 6 SERVINGS

new potato and radish salad with mustard-dill vinaigrette

cider vinegar,
6 tablespoons

cornichons, 7, minced

fresh dill, ¼ cup minced,
plus 2 tablespoons coarsely
chopped

shallot, 1, minced

dijon mustard,
3 tablespoons

sugar, 1 tablespoon

sea salt

extra-virgin olive oil,
½ cup plus 1 tablespoon

**red new potatoes, all about
the same size, 2** pounds

celery, 4 stalks, cut into
small dice

radishes, 8 large, trimmed
and cut into small dice

crème fraîche, ⅓ cup

MAKES 6 SERVINGS

In a small nonreactive bowl, whisk together the vinegar, cornichons, the ¼ cup minced dill, the shallot, mustard, sugar, and ½ teaspoon salt until the sugar dissolves. Slowly whisk in the olive oil until well blended to make a vinaigrette. Taste and adjust the seasonings.

Fill a large bowl two-thirds full with ice water. In a large saucepan, combine the potatoes, 1 tablespoon salt, and water to cover by 1 inch and bring to a boil over high heat. Reduce the heat to medium, cover partially, and simmer until the potatoes are just tender when pierced with the tip of a paring knife, 7–9 minutes.

Drain the potatoes in a colander and then immediately transfer them to the ice water. Let stand until cool, then drain again. Cut each potato into quarters and transfer to a large bowl.

Whisk the vinaigrette to recombine, then drizzle it over the potatoes. Add the celery and radishes and toss gently. Taste and adjust the seasonings. Transfer the salad to a serving bowl and sprinkle with the 2 tablespoons chopped dill. Serve right away, passing the crème fraîche for dolloping at the table.

Cornichons are tart, salty and full of pickled flavor. Along with the mustard, they add zip to the tender waxy potatoes and crunchy radishes and celery in this simple salad. A spoonful of crème fraîche on individual servings tempers the salad's tanginess and adds a luxurious touch.

Slices of tropical
pineapple soften
and caramelize on
a fiery grill. Their
sweetness and
bright acidity are
counterpoints to
rich, meaty leg of
lamb seasoned with
a profusion of sour,
sweet, spicy, salty,
and highly aromatic
ingredients—a
delicious layering
of vibrant flavors.

grilled lamb and pineapple salad with lemongrass and mint

boneless butterflied leg of lamb, 2¼ pounds, trimmed

lemongrass-mint paste (page 144)

fresh lime juice, ¼ cup

rice vinegar, 1 tablespoon

asian fish sauce, 1½ teaspoons

jalapeño chile, ½ teaspoon minced

light brown sugar, 3 tablespoons firmly packed

fresh mint, 3 tablespoons minced

sea salt and freshly ground pepper

canola oil

pineapple, 1

peanuts, 1 cup, toasted (page 145) and chopped

red leaf lettuce, 2 heads, leaves torn into bite-sized pieces

green onions, 8, thinly sliced

MAKES 6 SERVINGS

Lay the lamb in a large baking dish and rub the herb paste into both sides of the meat. Cover and refrigerate for at least 6 hours or preferably overnight.

In a small nonreactive bowl, whisk together the lime juice, vinegar, fish sauce, chile, sugar, mint, ½ teaspoon salt, and several grinds of pepper until the sugar dissolves. Slowly whisk in 5 tablespoons canola oil until well blended to make a dressing. Taste and adjust the seasonings. Set aside.

About 1 hour before serving, remove the lamb from the refrigerator. Using a chef's knife, peel the pineapple (page 145) and cut it crosswise into rounds about ¼ inch thick. Brush the pineapple on both sides with a little canola oil and season lightly with salt. Prepare a charcoal or gas grill for direct-heat cooking over medium-high heat (page 147).

Grill the pineapple, turning once, until grill-marked on both sides, 5–7 minutes total. Transfer to a cutting board. Scrape the paste off the lamb and lightly season both sides of the meat with salt. Grill, turning once, until an instant-read thermometer inserted into the thickest part of the meat registers 130°F for medium-rare, about 10 minutes total, or until done to your liking. Transfer to the cutting board and tent with aluminum foil. Cut each pineapple round into quarters and trim away the tough core from each piece.

In a small bowl, stir together the peanuts and ½ teaspoon salt. In a large bowl, toss the lettuce with ¼ teaspoon salt and several grinds of pepper. Whisk the dressing to recombine, then drizzle about half of it over the lettuce and toss well. Taste and adjust the seasonings. Divide the dressed lettuce evenly among individual plates.

Thinly slice the lamb. Arrange the lamb and pineapple on the salads, dividing them evenly, then drizzle each serving with some of the remaining dressing. Sprinkle with the peanuts and green onions and serve right away.

The citrusy scent and light, fresh flavor of lemongrass permeate this dish, whose Thai inspiration is revealed by the addition of mint, lime juice, and pungent fish sauce. A few minutes on a hot grill gives both the lamb and pineapple a smokiness that adds to the salad's wonderful complexity.

summer

caesar-style salad with poblano chiles and cornmeal croutons

unsalted butter,
2 tablespoons, at room temperature

chicken broth, 2 cups

sea salt and freshly ground pepper

yellow cornmeal, 1 cup

extra-virgin olive oil,
2 tablespoons

chili powder, ½ teaspoon

poblano chiles, 2

mayonnaise, ½ cup

fresh lime juice,
1 tablespoon

garlic, 1 large clove, minced

honey, 1½ teaspoons

dijon mustard, ½ teaspoon

romaine lettuce, 2 heads, leaves torn into bite-sized pieces

dry jack cheese, ¼ pound

MAKES 4–6 SERVINGS

Coat the inside of an 8-inch square baking dish with 1 tablespoon of the butter. In a saucepan over medium-high heat, bring the broth, ½ teaspoon salt, and the remaining 1 tablespoon butter to a boil. Reduce the heat to medium. Gradually add the cornmeal in a slow, steady stream while whisking constantly. Continue cooking and whisking until the mixture has thickened and pulls away from the sides of the pan, about 6 minutes. Immediately pour the mixture into the prepared baking dish, spreading it evenly. Cover and refrigerate until firm, about 1 hour.

Preheat the oven to 350°F. Cut the chilled cornmeal mixture into 1½-inch croutons. Transfer the croutons to a rimmed baking sheet, drizzle with the olive oil, sprinkle with the chili powder and ¼ teaspoon salt, and toss to coat. Bake until the croutons are dark gold and aromatic, about 30 minutes, shaking the pan after 10 minutes. Let cool to room temperature.

Preheat the broiler. Place the chiles on a rimmed baking sheet, place under the broiler, and broil, turning occasionally, until the skins are charred, about 10 minutes. Transfer to a bowl, cover, and let steam for 15 minutes. Remove and discard the skins, stems, and seeds and cut the flesh into small dice.

In a food processor, combine the mayonnaise, 2 tablespoons of the diced chiles, the lime juice, garlic, honey, mustard, ½ teaspoon salt, and several grinds of pepper and process until a smooth dressing forms, about 20 seconds. Taste and adjust the seasonings.

In a large bowl, toss the lettuce with ¼ teaspoon salt. Drizzle with about two-thirds of the dressing and toss well (reserve the remaining dressing for another use). Divide the dressed lettuce evenly among individual plates. Top each serving with cornmeal croutons and some of the remaining diced chiles. Using a vegetable peeler, shave the cheese over the salads, dividing it evenly. Serve right away.

The salty sharpness and rich, aged flavor of dry Jack cheese adds character to this Southwestern riff on classic Caesar salad. Roasted poblanos lend an earthy, green flavor and just a suggestion of heat, while the chili powder–spiced croutons offer substance and notes of toasty corn.

quinoa with tomatoes, cucumber, and fresh herbs

The trio of green onion, parsley, and mint brings an abundance of verdant flavor and a bold herbal taste to this salad inspired by traditional Middle Eastern tabbouleh. Quinoa is an earthy backdrop for summery vegetables and a dressing made with fruity olive oil and tangy-sweet pomegranate molasses.

In a saucepan, combine the quinoa, broth, and ¼ teaspoon salt and bring to a boil over high heat. Cover, reduce the heat to medium-low, and simmer until all of the liquid has been absorbed and the quinoa is tender, about 12 minutes. Immediately transfer the quinoa to a fine-mesh sieve and rinse with a fine stream of cold running water, making sure the water and quinoa don't overflow, until cooled, 1–2 minutes. Drain well, then transfer to a bowl.

Finely grate the zest from 1 lemon, then halve both lemons and juice the halves to measure 5 tablespoons. In a small nonreactive bowl, whisk together the lemon juice and zest, garlic, pomegranate molasses, sugar, ½ teaspoon salt, and several grinds of pepper until the sugar dissolves. Slowly whisk in the olive oil until well blended to make a dressing. Taste and adjust the seasonings. Add about three-fourths of the dressing to the quinoa and stir well.

Core the tomatoes and halve them crosswise. Gently squeeze each half to ease out the seeds, then cut the tomato flesh into ½-inch dice. In a small bowl, toss the tomatoes with ¼ teaspoon salt and let stand until they release their juice, about 5 minutes. Pour into a sieve set over a second bowl. Cut the cucumber into ½-inch dice and add it to the bowl you used to season the tomatoes. Add the green onions and the remaining dressing to the cucumber, toss well, then pour the cucumber mixture over the tomatoes in the sieve to drain. Add the drained tomato-cucumber mixture to the quinoa and stir in the parsley and mint. Taste and adjust the seasonings. Transfer to a serving bowl and serve right away.

quinoa, 1½ cups, rinsed and drained

chicken or vegetable broth, 3 cups

sea salt and freshly ground pepper

lemons, 2 large

garlic, 2 cloves, minced

pomegranate molasses, 1 tablespoon

sugar, 1 teaspoon

extra-virgin olive oil, ½ cup

tomatoes, 2 large

english cucumber, ½ large

green onions, 4, white and light green parts thinly sliced

fresh flat-leaf parsley, ¼ cup coarsely chopped

fresh mint, ¼ cup coarsely chopped

MAKES 4–6 SERVINGS

In a refreshing summer salad, ribbons of celery form a tangle with chunks of watermelon, bits of ricotta salata cheese, and mint leaves. An unusual dish, to be sure, but one with a delightful mix of sweet, salty, and cool herbal flavors.

watermelon and shaved celery with ricotta salata

celery, 6 stalks

seedless watermelon,
1 small (about 3¾ pounds)

ricotta salata **cheese,**
5–6 ounces, coarsely
crumbled

fresh mint leaves, 1 cup
torn

extra-virgin olive oil,
¼ cup

fresh lemon juice,
1 tablespoon

**sea salt and freshly ground
pepper**

MAKES 4–6 SERVINGS

If the celery stalks are fibrous, using a vegetable peeler, peel off and discard the stringy outer layer. Then, using the vegetable peeler, shave the stalks into long, thin strips. If they become too thin to shave, slice them as thinly as possible with a chef's knife.

Using the chef's knife, cut the watermelon in half through the stem end. Cut each half in half again to make quarters. Working with 1 quarter at a time, cut the flesh from the rind, carefully following the curve of the rind. Discard the rind and cut the flesh into ¾-inch cubes.

In a large bowl, combine the shaved celery, watermelon, cheese, and mint. Drizzle with the olive oil and lemon juice, sprinkle with 1 teaspoon salt and ¼ teaspoon pepper, and toss to mix well. Taste and adjust the seasonings. Using a slotted spoon, divide the salad evenly among chilled individual plates. Serve right away.

In this eye-catching salad, the saltiness and tangy, milky taste of ricotta salata *contrast deliciously against melon's sweet juiciness and celery's refreshing crunch. A handful of torn mint leaves adds coolness, while rich olive oil pulls all the flavors together.*

grilled eggplant, corn, and bread salad with tomato-basil vinaigrette

In this nontraditional take on classic Italian bread salad, basil is a fitting flavoring for a fresh tomato vinaigrette. More surprisingly, basil's sweet anise-like hints perfectly accent the smokiness of the grilled eggplant and toasty flavor of the charred corn.

Bring a saucepan two-thirds full with water to a boil over high heat. Fill a bowl two-thirds full with ice water. Using a paring knife, score an X on the bottom of each tomato. Drop the tomatoes into the boiling water and heat until the skins loosen, 15–30 seconds. Using a slotted spoon, transfer the tomatoes to the ice water and let stand until cool. Remove the tomatoes from the ice water and pull off the skins. Core the tomatoes and halve them crosswise. Gently squeeze each half to ease out the seeds, then coarsely chop the tomato flesh. You should have about 1½ cups chopped tomatoes.

Transfer the chopped tomatoes to a nonreactive bowl. Add 2 tablespoons of the basil, the vinegar, 1 tablespoon of the olive oil, the garlic, ½ teaspoon salt, and several grinds of pepper. Using an immersion blender, process until a chunky vinaigrette forms. (Or, pulse the ingredients in a standing blender.) Taste and adjust the seasonings. Set aside.

Prepare a charcoal or gas grill for direct-heat cooking over medium-high heat (page 147). Remove the husks and silk from the corn. Brush the ears on all sides with 1 tablespoon of the olive oil and season with salt and pepper. Brush the eggplant slices on both sides with the remaining 6 tablespoons olive oil and season both sides with salt and pepper.

Grill the eggplant slices, turning once, until softened and grill-marked on both sides, about 12 minutes total. Transfer to a cutting board. Grill the corn, turning frequently, until charred in spots, 10–12 minutes. Transfer to the cutting board. Cut the eggplant slices into ¾-inch pieces. Using a chef's knife, cut the ears of corn in half crosswise. Stand each half flat end down on a cutting board and cut the kernels from the cob.

In a large bowl, combine the eggplant, corn, the remaining 4 tablespoons basil, and the bread cubes. Pour in the tomato vinaigrette and toss well. Transfer to a platter or serving bowl and serve right away.

ripe tomatoes, 2 large (about 1 pound total weight)

fresh basil leaves, 6 tablespoons cut into thin ribbons

balsamic vinegar, 2 tablespoons

extra-virgin olive oil, 8 tablespoons

garlic, 2 large cloves, minced

sea salt and freshly ground pepper

corn, 3 ears

eggplant, 2 large (about 2½ pounds total weight), cut crosswise into slices ½ inch thick

***pane* pugliese or other coarse country bread,** 1 loaf (¾ pound), cut into 1-inch cubes (4 cups)

MAKES 6–8 SERVINGS

In a variation on classic salade niçoise, fatty wild salmon meets a handful of farmers' market vegetables, haricots verts among them. The slender green beans, cooked briefly so that they retain a subtle snap, bring their fresh, grassy flavor to the hearty salad.

salade niçoise with seared wild salmon

small red potatoes,
2 pounds, quartered

sea salt and freshly ground pepper

haricots verts, ¾ pound

wild salmon, 6 skinless fillets (5–6 ounces each), pin bones removed (page 147)

canola oil, 1 tablespoon

romaine lettuce, 1 head, thinly sliced

olive-anchovy vinaigrette (page 144)

grape or cherry tomatoes, 3½ cups, halved lengthwise

large eggs, 6, hard-cooked (page 144), peeled and cut into quarters

fresh chives, 2 tablespoons finely chopped

MAKES 6 SERVINGS

Fill a large bowl two-thirds full with ice water. In a large saucepan, combine the potatoes, 1 tablespoon salt, and water to cover by 1 inch and bring to a boil over high heat. Reduce the heat to medium, cover partially, and simmer until the potatoes are just tender when pierced with the tip of a paring knife, 5–7 minutes. Drain and immediately transfer the potatoes to the ice water. Let stand until cool and then use a slotted spoon to transfer the potatoes to a large bowl. Reserve the ice water bath.

Fill the same saucepan two-thirds full with water and bring to a boil over high heat. Add 1 tablespoon salt and the haricots verts and cook until tender-crisp, about 2 minutes. Drain and immediately transfer the beans to the ice water. Let stand until cool and drain well. Add the beans to the bowl with the potatoes. Set aside

Season the salmon fillets on both sides with salt and pepper. In a large nonstick frying pan, warm the canola oil over medium-high heat until very hot but not smoking. Working in batches, add the salmon pieces, skinned side up, and cook until golden brown, about 2 minutes. Turn the salmon over and cook until just opaque at the center, 2–3 minutes longer. Transfer to a large plate and tent with aluminum foil.

Add the lettuce, ¾ teaspoon salt, and several grinds of pepper to the potatoes and beans and toss to mix. Drizzle with about half of the vinaigrette and toss again. In a bowl, toss the tomatoes with ¼ teaspoon salt.

Divide the lettuce-potato-bean mixture evenly among individual plates. Using a slotted spoon, top each serving with an equal amount of the tomatoes, and then with a piece of salmon. Arrange 4 egg quarters on each serving and sprinkle them lightly with salt. Sprinkle each salad with chives and serve right away. Pass the remaining vinaigrette at the table.

Tiny Niçoise olives are briny, to be sure, but they also boast a meaty, slightly nutty flavor that is unique to the variety. Here, they're combined with anchovies and incorporated into the vinaigrette. The resulting dressing has a bold, assertive taste that easily stands up to the richness of the salmon.

shaved zucchini with lemon, mint, and feta

Cool, refreshing mint brightens this simple salad, in which shaved raw zucchini resembles wide ribbons of pasta. The zucchini's gentle squash flavor is punctuated by the salty tang of feta cheese. Olive oil infuses the dish with richness, and lemon zest adds citrusy notes.

Trim the zucchini but do not peel (the skin will add color and texture). Using a sharp vegetable peeler, shave the zucchini lengthwise into long, thin strips, letting the strips fall into a bowl. You should have about 6 cups. (Don't worry if you are unable to shave the seedy cores; discard them or reserve for another use.)

In a small bowl, whisk together the olive oil and lemon zest. Drizzle this mixture over the zucchini and season with ¼ teaspoon each of salt and pepper. Add the mint and feta to the bowl and toss gently. Taste and adjust the seasonings. Transfer the salad to a platter and serve right away.

zucchini, 4 (about 2 pounds total weight)

extra-virgin olive oil, ¼ cup

lemon zest, 1 teaspoon finely grated

coarse sea salt and freshly ground pepper

fresh mint leaves, ¼ cup torn

feta cheese, ⅓ pound, coarsely chopped

MAKES 4–6 SERVINGS

orzo salad with grape tomatoes, capers, and roasted garlic

garlic, 1 head

extra-virgin olive oil,
½ cup plus
1½ tablespoons

red wine vinegar, ¼ cup

sugar, 1 teaspoon

**sea salt and freshly ground
pepper**

orzo pasta, 2 cups
(¾ pound)

**grape tomatoes, preferably
a mixture of red and
yellow,** 4 cups, halved
lengthwise

capers, ¼ cup, rinsed and
drained

finely grated lemon zest,
1 tablespoon

fresh basil leaves, ½ cup
torn

MAKES 4–6 SERVINGS

Preheat the oven to 400°F.

Slice off the top ½ inch of the garlic head. Set the garlic head cut side up on a piece of aluminum foil large enough to enclose it completely, drizzle it with ½ tablespoon of the olive oil, and enclose tightly in the foil. Bake until golden brown and soft when gently squeezed, about 1 hour. Unwrap and let cool to room temperature.

Squeeze the roasted garlic cloves from the skins; discard the skins. Measure 2 tablespoons roasted garlic (reserve the remainder for another use) and place in a small nonreactive bowl. Add the vinegar, sugar, ½ teaspoon salt, and several grinds of pepper and whisk until the sugar dissolves. Slowly whisk in the remaining ½ cup plus 1 tablespoon olive oil until well blended to make a dressing. Taste and adjust the seasonings.

Bring a large saucepan two-thirds full with water to a boil over high heat. Add 1 tablespoon salt and the orzo, stir well, and cook until al dente, about 8 minutes, or according to package instructions. Drain in a colander and rinse with cold running water. Drain well again and transfer to a large bowl

In a bowl, toss the tomatoes with ½ teaspoon salt and let stand until they release their juice, about 5 minutes, then drain in a sieve. Add the drained tomatoes to the pasta along with about two-thirds of the dressing (reserve the remainder for another use), ¼ teaspoon salt, the capers, lemon zest, and basil. Taste and adjust the seasonings. Toss well, transfer to a serving bowl, and serve right away.

Capers are small in size, but they're big in flavor. They dot this salad of rice-like orzo pasta, their briny and piquant salt-and-vinegar taste offering a welcome contrast to sweet grape tomatoes, licorice-like basil, and nutty roasted garlic.

A marinade for steak reflects the layering of flavors in a main-course salad. With grilled flank steak and vibrant peppers as the stars, the dish is both colorful and delicious. A Spanish-influenced sauce acts as a dressing, adding a richness to tie the elements together.

grilled steak, pepper, and onion salad with romesco dressing

beef flank steak, 2¾ pounds

smoked paprika marinade (page 144)

red onions, 2 small

bell peppers, 3 (1 *each* yellow, red, and orange)

extra-virgin olive oil, 4 tablespoons

sea salt and freshly ground pepper

fresh orange juice, 1 tablespoon

sherry vinegar, 2 tablespoons

spanish sweet smoked paprika, ¼ teaspoon

garlic, 2 cloves, minced

jarred *piquillo* peppers, 3

blanched almonds, 1½ tablespoons chopped

green leaf lettuce, ½ large head, leaves torn into bite-sized pieces

fresh flat-leaf parsley, 2 tablespoons chopped

MAKES 6 SERVINGS

Lay the flank steak in a nonreactive baking dish and add the marinade. Turn the steak a few times to coat it with the marinade, cover, and refrigerate for at least 2 hours or preferably overnight, turning once or twice.

About 1 hour before cooking, remove the flank steak from the refrigerator. Cut the onions crosswise into rounds ½ inch thick (do not separate the layers). Cut the bell peppers into wide planks, removing and discarding the stems, seeds, and ribs. Brush the vegetables with 2 tablespoons of the olive oil and then season lightly with salt and pepper.

Prepare a charcoal or gas grill for direct-heat grilling over medium-high heat (page 147). While the grill heats, in a food processor, combine the remaining 2 tablespoons olive oil, the orange juice, vinegar, paprika, garlic, *piquillo* peppers, almonds, a scant ½ teaspoon salt, and a few grinds of pepper. Process until a relatively smooth dressing forms, about 15 seconds. Taste and adjust the seasonings. Set aside.

Grill the onions and peppers, turning once, until softened and lightly charred on both sides, 7–10 minutes for the onions and about 15 minutes for the peppers. Transfer to a plate. Remove the meat from the marinade and season both sides with salt and pepper. Grill, turning once, until browned on both sides and an instant-read thermometer inserted into the thickest part registers 130°F for medium rare, 10 15 minutes total, or until cooked to your liking. Transfer to a cutting board and tent with aluminum foil. Cut the peppers into ½-inch-wide strips and separate the onion slices into rings.

In a bowl, toss the lettuce with ⅛ teaspoon salt. Divide the lettuce evenly among individual plates. Thinly slice the steak on the diagonal. Top each mound of lettuce with an equal amount of the steak, onion, and peppers. Spoon the dressing over each salad, dividing evenly, and sprinkle with a little parsley. Serve right away.

Spanish smoked paprika is rich with earthy nuances of chiles, cocoa, and leather. In this recipe, it lends a robust smokiness and gorgeous red color to a steak marinade and romesco-style dressing. It's an apt seasoning for a dish brimming with charred flavors from the grill.

potato and green bean salad with herbs and anchovies

Anchovies provide a salty, savory backbone in this Provence-inspired dish. Their assertiveness is complemented by the pungency of mustard and garlic, and is tempered by the freshness of verdant herbs. Green beans and potatoes are mellow counterpoints to the bold dressing, but their flavors come through beautifully.

Bring a saucepan two-thirds full of water to a boil over high heat. Fill a large bowl two-thirds full with ice water. Add 1 tablespoon salt and the green beans to the boiling water and cook until bright green and just tender-crisp, about 4 minutes. Drain the beans and immediately transfer them to the ice water. Let stand until cool, then drain again. Cut each green bean in half crosswise and set aside.

In the same saucepan used to cook the green beans, combine the potatoes, 1½ tablespoons salt, and water to cover by 1 inch and bring to a boil over high heat. Reduce the heat to medium, cover partially, and simmer until the potatoes are just tender when pierced with the tip of a knife, 8–10 minutes. Drain in a colander and let stand until cool enough to handle. Cut the potatoes into slices ⅜ inch thick and transfer to a large bowl.

In a food processor, combine the anchovies, shallots, and garlic and pulse until minced, about 5 one-second pulses. Add the sugar, mustard, basil, tarragon, parsley, vinegar, and oilve oil and process until a relatively smooth dressing forms, about 10 seconds. Taste and adjust the seasonings.

Add about three-fourths of the dressing to the warm potatoes and toss well to coat. Add the green beans, the remaining dressing, 1¼ teaspoons salt, and ¼ teaspoon pepper and toss well. Taste and adjust the seasonings. Transfer to a serving bowl and serve right away. Or, for fuller flavor, let stand at room temperature for about 1 hour before serving.

sea salt and freshly ground pepper

green beans, 1 pound

small potatoes, preferably yukon gold, 3 pounds

olive oil–packed anchovy fillets, 6 or 7

shallots, 2 small

garlic, 1 large clove

sugar, ½ teaspoon

dijon mustard, 1 teaspoon

fresh basil leaves, ½ cup

fresh tarragon leaves, ½ cup

fresh flat-leaf parsley leaves, ½ cup

white wine vinegar, 6 tablespoons

extra-virgin olive oil, ¾ cup

MAKES 6–8 SERVINGS

antipasto salad with peperoncini vinaigrette

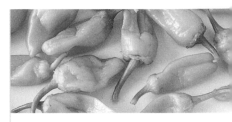

extra-virgin olive oil,
¼ cup, plus 6 tablespoons

garlic, 4 cloves, minced

sourdough baguette, 1

sea salt

red wine vinegar, ¼ cup

peperoncini, 5, stemmed,
seeded, and minced

fresh oregano,
1 tablespoon finely
chopped

sugar, 2 teaspoons

cherry or grape tomatoes,
preferably a mixture of red
and yellow, 4 cups, halved
lengthwise

hass avocados, 3

arugula leaves, 1–2 cups,
stems removed

provolone cheese,
½ pound, cut into ½-inch
cubes

prosciutto, ⅔ pound thinly
sliced

MAKES 6 SERVINGS

Preheat the oven to 350°F.

In a bowl, mix together the ¼ cup olive oil and the garlic. Cut the baguette into 18 slices each about ½ inch thick and arrange in a single layer on a baking sheet. Brush both sides of the baguette slices with the garlic oil and sprinkle lightly with salt. Bake until slightly crisp but not browned, about 10 minutes. Let cool to room temperature.

In a small nonreactive bowl, whisk together the vinegar, minced *peperoncini,* oregano, sugar, and ¼ teaspoon salt until the sugar dissolves. Slowly whisk in the 6 tablespoons olive oil until well blended to make a vinaigrette. Taste and adjust the seasonings.

In a bowl, toss the tomatoes with ¼ teaspoon salt and let stand until they release their juice, about 5 minutes, then drain in a sieve. Halve, pit, and peel the avocados (pages 145–146) and cut them crosswise into slices about ⅜ inch thick. Sprinkle the avocados with a large pinch of salt.

Arrange the arugula, drained tomatoes, avocados, and cheese on a large platter. Whisk the vinaigrette to recombine, then drizzle it over the arranged components. Arrange the prosciutto and sourdough toasts on the platter and serve right away.

An Italian deli sandwich is the inspiration for this lively dressing. Its spicy, vinegary heat from minced peperoncini is a foil for buttery avocado, silky prosciutto, and creamy provolone. Toasted slices of garlicky sourdough bread are the ideal accompaniment to the free-form salad.

Peaches caramelized on a grill take on an intensified sweetness. Here, they're paired with sharp blue cheese and mild butter lettuce. A raspberry vinaigrette complements the peaches' fruitiness and balances the piquancy of the cheese.

grilled peach salad with blue cheese and raspberry vinaigrette

raspberries, ½ cup

fresh orange juice,
3 tablespoons

raspberry vinegar,
1½ teaspoons

sugar, 1½ teaspoons

sea salt and freshly ground pepper

extra-virgin olive oil,
3 tablespoons, plus oil for brushing

peaches, 3, halved and pitted

canola oil for grilling

honey, 1 tablespoon

shelled pistachio nuts,
½ cup, toasted (page 145)

butter lettuce, 1½ small heads, leaves separated

blue cheese, such as maytag, ¼ pound, crumbled

MAKES 4 SERVINGS

In a blender, combine the raspberries and orange juice and process until smooth, about 10 seconds. Strain through a fine-mesh sieve into a small nonreactive bowl, pressing on the solids to extract as much purée as possible. Whisk in the vinegar, sugar, ⅛ teaspoon salt, and several grinds of pepper until the sugar dissolves. Slowly whisk in the 3 tablespoons olive oil until well blended to make a vinaigrette. Taste and adjust the seasonings.

Prepare a charcoal or gas grill for direct-heat cooking over medium-high heat (page 147). Alternatively, preheat a ridged grill pan on the stove top over medium-high heat.

Brush the peach halves on both sides with olive oil. Lightly season on both sides with salt and pepper.

Brush the hot grill rack or grill pan with canola oil. Grill the peach halves, turning once, until softened and grill-marked on both sides, 2–3 minutes total. Transfer to a cutting board and brush the cut sides evenly with the honey. Cut each peach half into quarters.

In a small bowl, stir together the pistachios and ⅛ teaspoon salt. In a large bowl, toss the lettuce with a generous ⅛ teaspoon salt and several grinds of pepper. Whisk the vinaigrette to recombine, then drizzle half of it over the lettuce and toss well. Divide the dressed lettuce evenly among individual plates. Top each salad with the peach pieces, dividing them evenly, then sprinkle with the pistachios and blue cheese. Drizzle each salad with some of the remaining vinaigrette and serve right away.

Here, plump fresh raspberries are made into a vibrant dressing with floral hints from the berries and a light acidity from orange juice and raspberry vinegar. Crunchy pistachios play off the tenderness of grilled peaches, while the salty blue cheese contrasts against the salad's sweet, fruity flavors.

fall

roasted mushroom and shallot salad with balsamic vinaigrette

mixed wild and cultivated mushrooms such as chanterelle and shiitake, 1 pound

extra-virgin olive oil, 8 tablespoons, plus 2 teaspoons

fresh thyme leaves, 2½ teaspoons

sea salt and freshly ground pepper

shallots, 4 large

balsamic vinegar, ¼ cup

fresh lemon juice, 1 teaspoon

sugar, ½ teaspoon

treviso radicchio, 1 head, thinly sliced

red leaf lettuce, 1 small head, leaves torn into bite-sized pieces

fresh flat-leaf parsley, 1 cup coarsely chopped

MAKES 6 SERVINGS

Preheat the oven to 400°F. Trim off and discard the tough stems from the mushrooms, and then thinly slice them.

On a small rimmed baking sheet, toss together the mushrooms, 3 tablespoons of the olive oil, 2 teaspoons of the thyme, ½ teaspoon salt, and ¼ teaspoon pepper. In a pie pan or small baking dish, toss together the shallots, the 2 teaspoons olive oil, 2 pinches of salt, and several grinds of pepper. Place both pans in the oven. Roast the mushrooms until golden brown and tender, about 15 minutes, stirring once halfway through cooking. Roast the shallots until soft and lightly browned, 25–30 minutes, stirring once halfway through cooking. Trim off and discard the root ends of 2 of the roasted shallots and add them to a food processor. Cover the remaining shallots and the mushrooms with aluminum foil to keep warm.

Add the remaining 5 tablespoons olive oil, the remaining ½ teaspoon thyme, the vinegar, lemon juice, sugar, a scant ½ teaspoon salt, and several grinds of pepper to the food processor and process until a smooth dressing forms, about 30 seconds. Taste and adjust the seasonings.

Thinly slice the remaining 2 roasted shallots. In a large bowl, toss together the radicchio, lettuce, parsley, 2 pinches of salt, and several grinds of pepper. Drizzle with about two-thirds of the dressing and toss again. Taste and adjust the seasonings. Divide the dressed greens evenly among individual plates. Top each serving with an equal amount of the warm mushrooms and sliced shallots and drizzle with some of the remaining dressing. Serve right away.

Used both in the dressing and as a salad component, roasted shallots suffuse this dish with their sweet, mellow, onionlike flavor. The roasted mushrooms bring a savory earthiness that pairs nicely with the shallots and the bitterness of the radicchio.

farro salad with turkey, dried cranberries, and roasted squash

In this grain-based salad, sweet-and-sour dried cranberries contrast with smoked turkey and earthy butternut squash. Lemon juice and green onions add freshness, while the nutty taste of farro serves as a neutral flavor backdrop. The result is a dish with an inviting fall spirit and a wonderful layering of tastes and textures.

Place the *farro* in a bowl and add water to cover. Let soak for 30 minutes.

Drain the *farro* in a sieve, transfer to a saucepan, add the broth and 1 teaspoon salt, and bring to a boil over high heat. Reduce the heat to medium-low and simmer, uncovered, until the *farro* is tender and all of the liquid is absorbed, about 30 minutes. Transfer to a large bowl and let cool to room temperature.

Meanwhile, preheat the oven to 400°F. Peel the squash, cut it in half lengthwise, and scoop out the seeds and strings. Cut the flesh into ½-inch cubes; you should have about 4½ cups. On a rimmed baking sheet, toss the squash cubes with 2 tablespoons of the olive oil, a generous teaspoon of salt, and a generous ¼ teaspoon pepper. Spread the cubes in an even layer on the baking sheet and roast until tender but still slightly firm to the bite, about 12 minutes. Let cool to room temperature.

In a small nonreactive bowl, whisk together the lemon juice, honey, parsley, ¼ teaspoon salt, and several grinds of pepper. Slowly whisk in the remaining 6 tablespoons olive oil until well blended to make a dressing. Taste and adjust the seasonings.

Add the dressing, squash, turkey, cranberries, and green onions to the cooled *farro* and toss well. Transfer to a serving bowl and serve right away.

farro, 1⅓ cups (about ½ pound)

low-sodium chicken broth, 4 cups

sea salt and freshly ground pepper

butternut squash, 1 (about 3 pounds)

extra-virgin olive oil, 8 tablespoons

fresh lemon juice, ¼ cup

honey, 1 teaspoon

fresh flat-leaf parsley, 1 tablespoon minced

boneless smoked turkey, 6 ounces, cut into ½-inch cubes

sweetened dried cranberries, ⅔ cup

green onions, 3, white and light green parts thinly sliced

MAKES 6 SERVINGS

Before they disappear, enjoy fresh figs in this elegant autumn salad. Against the bitterness of escarole and the nuttiness of aged Gouda, figs' honeyed notes shine brilliantly. A Port wine dressing completes the dish with a sweet-tart intensity.

escarole and figs with ruby port dressing

ruby port, 1 cup

balsamic vinegar, ¼ cup

sugar, ¼ teaspoon

sea salt and freshly ground pepper

extra-virgin olive oil, ¼ cup

escarole, 1 head, leaves torn into bite-sized pieces

mission figs, 10–12, stemmed and halved lengthwise

aged gouda cheese, ¼ pound

MAKES 4–6 SERVINGS

In a small, heavy saucepan over medium-high heat, simmer the Port until syrupy and reduced to ¼ cup, about 15 minutes. Remove from the heat and let cool to room temperature.

In a small nonreactive bowl, whisk together the reduced Port, balsamic vinegar, sugar, 2 pinches of salt, and a pinch of pepper until the sugar dissolves. Slowly whisk in the olive oil until well blended to make a dressing. Taste and adjust the seasonings.

In a large bowl, toss the escarole with 2 big pinches of salt and several grinds of pepper. Whisk the dressing to recombine, then drizzle about half of it over the escarole and toss well. Taste and adjust the seasonings. Divide the dressed escarole evenly among individual plates, and then top each serving with 4 or 5 fig halves. Using a vegetable peeler, shave the cheese over the salads, dividing it evenly. Drizzle each salad with some of the remaining dressing and serve right away.

Ruby Port has a sweet—but quite potent—flavor. Cooked down to a syrup and combined with balsamic vinegar, it forms an intense, dessert-like dressing for fresh figs, assertive escarole, and authentic Gouda cheese.

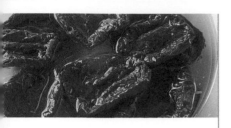

fennel, chickpea, and sun-dried tomato salad with mozzarella

Sun-dried tomatoes hold the concentrated essence of ripe tomatoes and have a chewy, meaty texture. In this salad, their intensity is kept in check by nutty chickpeas and milky, mild-tasting fresh mozzarella bocconcini. Slices of fennel add crunch and a licorice flavor, while fresh dill and oregano bring fragrant, herbal hints.

In a bowl, toss together the chickpeas, sun-dried tomatoes, 1 tablespoon of the olive oil, 2 tablespoons of the dill, the oregano, the 1 teaspoon lemon juice, ¼ teaspoon salt, and several grinds of pepper. Let stand at room temperature for 15 minutes.

In a small nonreactive bowl, whisk together the ¼ cup lemon juice, sugar, ¼ teaspoon salt, and several grinds of pepper until the sugar dissolves. Slowly whisk in the remaining 6 tablespoons olive oil until well blended to make a dressing. Taste and adjust the seasonings.

In a large bowl, toss together the fennel, lettuce, the remaining dill, ¼ teaspoon salt, and several grinds of pepper. Whisk the dressing to recombine, then drizzle it over the fennel-lettuce mixture and toss well. Taste and adjust the seasonings. Divide the dressed mixture evenly among individual plates. Top with the chickpea–sun-dried tomato mixture and the *boconccini*, dividing them evenly. Serve right away.

chickpeas, 1 can (15½ ounces), drained and rinsed

olive oil–packed sun-dried tomatoes, 1 cup drained, coarsely chopped

extra-virgin olive oil, 7 tablespoons

fresh dill, ⅔ cup finely chopped

fresh oregano, 1 teaspoon finely chopped

fresh lemon juice, ¼ cup, plus 1 teaspoon

sea salt and freshly ground pepper

sugar, 1 teaspoon

fennel bulbs, 2 small, cored and thinly sliced

romaine lettuce, 1 head, leaves torn into bite-sized pieces

fresh mozzarella *bocconcini*, 6 ounces, cut into quarters

MAKES 6 SERVINGS

A warm spinach salad is made heartier by the addition of gently poached farm-fresh eggs. Bits of crisp pancetta dot the greens, adding their salty allure, while thyme offers its woodsy fragrance. It's a perfect dish for an autumn brunch.

spinach salad with poached eggs and warm pancetta vinaigrette

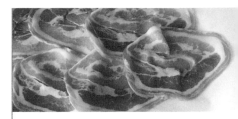

extra-virgin olive oil, 1 tablespoon, plus oil as needed for the vinaigrette

pancetta, ¼ pound, cut into ¼-inch cubes

raspberry or red wine vinegar, ½ cup

fresh thyme leaves, 2½ teaspoons

sugar, ½ teaspoon

shallots, 2 large, minced

sea salt and freshly ground pepper

spinach, 1 bunch (1 pound), stems removed

poached eggs (page 144)

MAKES 6 SERVINGS

Heat a small nonreactive sauté pan over medium-high heat until hot. Add the 1 tablespoon olive oil and heat until it ripples. Add the pancetta and cook, stirring occasionally, until browned and crisp, about 4 minutes. Pour into a sieve set over a small heatproof bowl and set aside.

In a small nonreactive bowl, whisk together the vinegar, thyme, and sugar until the sugar dissolves.

Return the sauté pan to medium-high heat (it will still be filmed with fat). Add the shallots and sauté until translucent and soft but not browned, about 1 minute. Add the vinegar mixture, bring to a boil, and boil for 1 minute, scraping up any browned bits from the pan bottom with a wooden spoon. Remove from the heat. Add several grinds of pepper and 3½ tablespoons of the reserved pancetta fat to the pan, supplementing with olive oil if needed. Whisk until well blended to make a vinaigrette. Taste and adjust the seasonings, then cover to keep warm.

In a large bowl, toss the spinach with 2 big pinches of salt and several grinds of pepper. Whisk the warm vinaigrette to recombine, then drizzle about half of it over the spinach and toss well. Taste and adjust the seasonings. Divide the dressed spinach evenly among individual plates. Top each serving with a poached egg. Drizzle each egg with some of the remaining vinaigrette and season very lightly with pepper. Scatter the cooked pancetta over the salads and serve right away.

This recipe features salty, savory pancetta in two ways: Its rendered fat lends a rich, meaty taste to the warm tart-sweet vinaigrette, and crisp, fried bits are scattered over the plated dish. A poached egg adds another element of richness to this satisfying salad.

mesclun and roasted pears with grainy mustard vinaigrette

Grainy mustard is a piquant counterpoint to the fruity undertones of the apple juice and cider vinegar in the dressing that coats this autumnal salad. Roasted pears give the salad substance and sweetness, and toasted pumpkin seeds add an appealing crunch.

Preheat the oven to 400°F.

Halve the pears through the stem end, and then core each half and cut lengthwise into slices about ½ inch thick. Place the slices on a rimmed baking sheet, drizzle with the 2 tablespoons olive oil, sprinkle with ¼ teaspoon salt, and toss to coat. Spread the slices in a single layer and roast for 20 minutes. Carefully turn the slices over and continue to roast until they are golden brown and tender but still hold their shape, about 20 minutes longer. Let cool to room temperature.

In a small nonreactive bowl, whisk together the vinegar, apple juice, shallot, mustard, brown sugar, ¼ teaspoon salt, and several grinds of pepper until the sugar dissolves. Slowly whisk in the remaining ¼ cup olive oil until well blended to make a dressing. Taste and adjust the seasonings.

In a small bowl, stir together the pumpkin seeds and a pinch of salt. In a large bowl, toss together the mesclun, endive leaves, a big pinch of salt, and several grinds of pepper. Whisk the dressing to recombine, then drizzle about half of it over the greens and toss well. Taste and adjust the seasonings. Divide the dressed greens evenly among individual plates. Arrange the roasted pear slices on top of the greens, dividing them evenly, and drizzle lightly with dressing (reserve any remaining dressing for another use). Sprinkle the pumpkin seeds over of the salads, dividing them evenly, and serve right away.

firm pears, preferably anjou or bosc, 3

extra-virgin olive oil, ¼ cup, plus 2 tablespoons

sea salt and freshly ground pepper

cider vinegar, ¼ cup

apple juice, 3 tablespoons

shallot, 1 large, minced

whole-grain mustard, 2 teaspoons

light brown sugar, 1½ teaspoons firmly packed

unsalted pumpkin seeds, 3 tablespoons, toasted (page 145)

mesclun, 4 heaping cups

belgian endives, 2 large, leaves separated

MAKES 6 SERVINGS

cabbage, asian pear, and grape salad with cider vinaigrette

cider vinegar,
2½ tablespoons

honey, 2 teaspoons

dijon mustard,
½ teaspoon

sea salt and freshly ground pepper

extra-virgin olive oil,
2½ tablespoons

asian pear, 1 large

red cabbage, ½ small head

seedless green grapes,
2 cups, halved

MAKES 6 SERVINGS

In a small nonreactive bowl, whisk together the vinegar, honey, mustard, ⅛ teaspoon salt, and a few grinds of pepper. Slowly whisk in the olive oil until well blended to make a vinaigrette. Taste and adjust the seasonings.

Halve and core the pear, and then cut the halves into thin strips. Cut the cabbage half lengthwise into 2 wedges, then cut away and discard the hard core from each wedge. Cut each wedge crosswise into thin shreds.

In a large bowl, gently toss together the pear, cabbage, grapes, ¼ teaspoon salt, and several grinds of pepper. Whisk the vinaigrette to recombine, then drizzle it over the pear-cabbage-grape mixture and toss well. Taste and adjust the seasonings. Transfer to a shallow bowl and serve right away.

Here, tart and slightly sweet cider vinegar teams up with honey and Dijon mustard to form a sprightly vinaigrette. It perfectly complements the fruitiness of the green grapes and crisp Asian pears in this fresh take on coleslaw.

broccoli and cauliflower salad with pickled onions and bacon

These pickled red onions are briskly tart and sweet and redolent of black pepper and cloves. They contrast beautifully in flavor and color with smoky, salty bacon and cabbage-like steamed broccoli and cauliflower for a simple and hearty cool-weather salad.

In a small, nonreactive saucepan, combine the vinegar, sugar, peppercorns, cloves, and ¼ teaspoon salt and bring to a boil over high heat. Reduce the heat to medium-low and simmer for 10 minutes to infuse the flavors. Pour the mixture into a heatproof nonreactive bowl, add the onion, and let stand at room temperature for 1 hour.

Meanwhile, in a large frying pan over medium heat, cook the bacon, turning once, until crisp and browned, about 7 minutes. Transfer to a paper towel–lined plate to drain. Let cool to room temperature, then coarsely chop.

Fill a large Dutch oven or other heavy pot with a lid with 1–2 inches of water, fit the pot with a steamer basket, and bring the water to a boil over high heat. Fill a large bowl two-thirds full with ice water and stir in 1 tablespoon salt until the salt dissolves. Place the cauliflower florets in a single layer in the steamer basket, cover, reduce the heat to medium, and steam until tender-crisp, about 8 minutes. Immediately transfer the cauliflower to the ice water. Let stand until cool, then use a slotted spoon to transfer the cauliflower florets to a large bowl. Reserve the ice water bath. Steam the broccoli florets in the same manner until tender-crisp, about 4 minutes, then transfer to the ice water until cool. Drain well and add to the bowl with the cauliflower.

Drizzle the olive oil over the cauliflower and broccoli, season with ¼ teaspoon salt and several grinds of pepper, and toss well. Taste and adjust the seasonings. Transfer to a serving bowl. Top with some of the pickled onion slices, lifting them out with a fork and removing any whole spices (reserve the remaining pickled onions for another use). Sprinkle with the bacon and serve right away.

cider vinegar, 2 cups

sugar, 3 tablespoons

black peppercorns, 16

whole cloves, 11

sea salt and freshly ground pepper

red onion, 1 large, thinly sliced

bacon, 5 slices

cauliflower, 1 head, cut into 1-inch florets (about 4 cups)

broccoli, 1 large head, cut into 1-inch florets (about 6 cups)

extra-virgin olive oil, ¼ cup

MAKES 6–8 SERVINGS

In the fall, freshly dug carrots fill farmers' markets, their textures crisp and their flavors sweet. Here, carrot-raisin salad is reinvented, made in part with earthy parsnips, North African spices, and the delicate nuttiness of pistachios.

north african–spiced carrot and parsnip salad

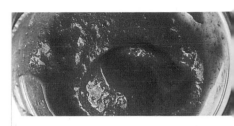

ground cinnamon,
¼ teaspoon

ground cumin,
¼ teaspoon

ground coriander,
¼ teaspoon

ground ginger,
⅛ teaspoon

carrots, 3 large (about
¾ **pound total weight)**

parsnips, 3 large (about
¾ **pound total weight)**

fresh lemon juice, ¼ cup

honey, 1 tablespoon

harissa, ¾ teaspoon

sea salt and freshly ground pepper

extra-virgin olive oil,
6 tablespoons

shelled pistachio nuts,
½ cup, toasted (page 145)
and coarsely chopped

raisins, ⅔ cup

fresh cilantro or mint,
¼ cup coarsely chopped

MAKES 6 SERVINGS

In a small, heavy frying pan over medium-low heat, toast the cinnamon, cumin, coriander, and ginger, stirring constantly, until fragrant, about 2 minutes. Remove from the heat and let cool to room temperature.

Peel the carrots and parsnips and shred them on the large holes of a box grater-shredder. Set aside.

In a small nonreactive bowl, whisk together the toasted spices, lemon juice, honey, *harissa,* and a scant ½ teaspoon salt. Slowly whisk in the olive oil until well blended to make a dressing. Taste and adjust the seasonings.

In a bowl, stir together the pistachios and a pinch of salt. Add the carrots and parsnips, raisins, ½ teaspoon salt, several grinds of pepper, and the dressing and toss well. Taste and adjust the seasonings. Transfer to a platter or serving bowl, sprinkle with the cilantro, and serve right away.

Harissa, *a North African pepper-and-spice paste, adds a suggestion of heat to this salad, a flavorful tangle of earthy and sweet ingredients. Toasted spices infuse the dish with their warmth, while the smooth richness of extra-virgin olive oil brings depth and harmonizes the flavors.*

hoisin-cashew chicken in lettuce cups

Salty-sweet hoisin sauce posesses a deep, spicy, molasses-like flavor. It's the defining ingredient in this easy-to-make ground chicken salad that is also fragrant with generous doses of ginger and garlic. Toasted cashews add both a delicious nuttiness and welcome crunch.

In a large frying pan over medium heat, warm the sesame oil. Add the onion, ginger, and garlic and sauté, stirring occasionally, until aromatic and the onion has softened, about 2 minutes. Add the ground chicken and raise the heat to medium-high. Cook, stirring and breaking up the meat with a wooden spoon, until the chicken is evenly crumbled, cooked through, and no longer pink, about 8 minutes.

Meanwhile, in a small bowl, whisk together the hoisin, tamari, *Sriracha* sauce, and brown sugar. When the chicken is ready, add the hoisin mixture and half of the cashews to the pan and cook, stirring occasionally, until aromatic, about 3 minutes. Remove from the heat and cover to keep warm.

In a large bowl, toss the lettuce with 2 pinches of salt and several grinds of pepper. Divide the lettuce leaves evenly among individual plates or arrange on a platter. Spoon the warm chicken mixture into the lettuce leaves, dividing it evenly. Garnish with the remaining cashews and the green onions and serve right away.

sesame oil, 2 tablespoons

yellow onion, ½, finely chopped

fresh ginger, 1½-inch piece, peeled and finely chopped

garlic, 7 large cloves, minced

ground chicken, 1½ pounds

hoisin sauce, ¾ cup

reduced-sodium tamari, 6 tablespoons

sriracha **sauce,** 1¼ teaspoons

light brown sugar, 2 teaspoons firmly packed

raw cashews, 1 cup, toasted (page 145) and roughly chopped

butter lettuce, 1 large head, separated into leaves

sea salt and freshly ground pepper

green onions, 3, white and light green parts thinly sliced

MAKES 6 SERVINGS

In a recipe celebrating the flavors of Mexico, a creamy dressing is brimming with smoky, spicy chipotle, tangy citrus juice, and pungent cilantro. Plump grilled shrimp make the salad a wonderful choice for an Indian-summer supper.

grilled shrimp salad with avocados and chipotle dressing

mayonnaise, ⅓ cup plus 1 tablespoon

fresh cilantro, ¾ cup coarsely chopped

fresh lime juice, 2½ tablespoons

fresh orange juice, 1½ tablespoons

shallot, 1 small, minced

chipotle chiles in adobo sauce, 1 tablespoon seeded and minced, plus 1½ tablespoons adobo sauce

sea salt and freshly ground pepper

large shrimp in the shell, 1½ pounds, peeled and deveined

black beans, 1 can (15 ounces), drained and rinsed

hass avocados, 2

romaine lettuce, 1 large head, leaves torn into bite-sized pieces

MAKES 6–8 SERVINGS

In a food processor, combine the mayonnaise, half of the cilantro, 2 teaspoons of the lime juice, the orange juice, minced shallot, the minced chipotle chile, ¼ teaspoon salt, and several grinds of pepper and process until a creamy, smooth dressing forms, about 10 seconds. Taste and adjust the seasonings. Cover and refrigerate until needed.

Soak 12 bamboo skewers in water to cover for at least 30 minutes. Prepare a charcoal or gas grill for direct-heat grilling over high heat (page 147).

In a bowl, combine the shrimp, 1 tablespoon of the lime juice, and 1 tablespoon of the adobo sauce and toss to coat evenly. Let stand at room temperature for 15 minutes to blend the flavors.

In a small bowl, combine the beans, the remaining ½ tablespoon adobo sauce, ½ teaspoon of the lime juice, ¼ teaspoon salt, and a few grinds of pepper. Let stand at room temperature for 15 minutes to blend the flavors.

Drain the skewers and thread 3 or 4 shrimp onto each skewer. Sprinkle lightly with salt and pepper and grill, turning once, until the shrimp are pink and opaque throughout, 3–5 minutes total. Transfer to a plate and sprinkle the shrimp with the remaining 2 teaspoons lime juice. Slide the shrimp off the skewers and set aside.

Halve, pit, and peel the avocados (pages 145–146) and cut them lengthwise into wedges about ⅜ inch thick.

In a large bowl, toss the lettuce with ¼ teaspoon salt and several grinds of pepper. Divide the lettuce evenly among individual plates. Top each serving with black beans, shrimp, and avocado wedges, dividing each element evenly. Drizzle each salad with about 2 tablespoons of the dressing and sprinkle with 1 tablespoon of the remaining cilantro. Serve right away.

In this salad, smoky canned chipotle chiles (smoked red jalapeño chiles) power the creamy citrus- and cilantro-laced dressing, while the tangy adobo sauce that the chiles are packed in seasons the other salad components. The shrimp acquire a charred flavor on the grill, accentuating the dressing's underlying smokiness. Avocados and black beans add mellow richness to the mix.

winter

arugula with oranges, marcona almonds, and pecorino

oranges, 4

honey, ½ teaspoon

sea salt and freshly ground pepper

peppery extra-virgin olive oil, 2 tablespoons

marcona almonds, ¾ cup, coarsely chopped

baby arugula, 6 cups

pecorino romano cheese, ⅓ pound

MAKES 4–6 SERVINGS

Working with 1 orange at a time, and using a thin-bladed knife, cut a thin slice off the top and bottom. Stand the fruit on a cut end, and working from top to bottom, cut away the peel and white pith in wide strips, following the contour of the fruit. Working over a bowl, slide the knife blade along both sides of each segment to free it from the membrane, capturing the segments and juice in the bowl. Repeat with the remaining oranges, then squeeze the membranes left behind to extract any additional juice.

Measure 3½ tablespoons of the orange juice and place in a small bowl (reserve the remainder for another use). Whisk in the honey, ⅛ teaspoon salt, and a few grinds of pepper. Slowly whisk in the olive oil until well blended to make a dressing. Taste and adjust the seasonings.

In a small bowl, stir together the almonds and ¼ teaspoon salt. Place the arugula in a large bowl. Whisk the dressing to recombine, then drizzle it over the arugula and toss well. Taste and adjust the seasonings. Divide the dressed arugula evenly among individual plates, mounding it in the center. Top each mound with the orange segments, dividing evenly, and sprinkle the oranges very lightly with salt. Scatter the almonds over the salads, dividing evenly. Using a vegetable peeler, shave the cheese over the salads, dividing evenly. Serve right away.

Large and flat in shape, and incredibly rich and toasty in flavor, Spanish Marcona almonds deliver crunch to this salad of bright oranges and salty-tangy cheese. Peppery extra-virgin olive oil adds a lusciousness that rounds out the contrasting tastes.

spicy pomelo salad with lime, mint, and basil

Lime juice adds bright acidity to this Southeast Asian—themed salad, an interplay of sweet, salty, sour, and spicy tastes. The bracing, grapefruit-like flavor of pomelo is the highlight, its citrusy freshness accented by fragrant mint and basil. If you can't find pomelos, white grapefruits are a suitable substitute.

In a small nonreactive bowl, whisk together the vinegar, lime juice, brown sugar, fish sauce, *Sriracha* sauce, shallot, and chile until the sugar dissolves. Slowly whisk in the canola oil until well blended to make a dressing. Taste and adjust the seasonings.

Working with 1 pomelo at a time, and using a thin-bladed knife, cut a thin slice off the top and bottom. Stand the fruit on a cut end, and working from top to bottom, cut away the peel and white pith in wide strips, following the contour of the fruit. Working over a bowl, slide the knife blade along both sides of each segment to free it from the membrane, capturing the segments in the bowl.

Pull off and discard any wilted outer leaves from the cabbage. Halve the head lengthwise and cut away the hard core from each half. Cut each half crosswise into thin slices.

In a small bowl, stir together the peanuts and ¼ teaspoon salt. In a large bowl, toss together the cabbage, carrots, mint, basil, and 2 pinches of salt. Whisk the dressing to recombine, then drizzle it over the cabbage-carrot mixture and toss well. Taste and adjust the seasonings. Divide the cabbage-carrot mixture evenly among individual plates and top with the pomelo segments, dividing them evenly. Lightly sprinkle the pomelo on each salad with salt and pepper and then scatter the peanuts on top. Serve right away.

rice vinegar, 2 tablespoons

fresh lime juice, 1½ tablespoons

light brown sugar, 1½ teaspoons firmly packed

asian fish sauce, 1¾ teaspoons

sriracha **sauce,** ½ teaspoon

shallot, 1 small, minced

jalapeño chile, ¼ teaspoon minced

canola oil, 3 tablespoons

pomelos, 3

napa cabbage, 1 head

roasted peanuts, ¾ cup coarsely chopped

sea salt and freshly ground pepper

carrots, 3 large, peeled and shredded

fresh mint, ½ cup chopped

fresh basil, ½ cup chopped

MAKES 6 SERVINGS

Candied walnuts are irresistible, their texture crisped in the oven and their bitterness tamed by a dusting of sugar. They bring a rich, indulgent quality to a salad with a trio of tangy elements: apples, goat cheese, and a lemony dressing.

apple salad with candied walnuts and roasted-lemon dressing

lemons, 3, halved

extra-virgin olive oil,
¼ cup, plus 2 teaspoons

large egg white, 1

walnut halves and pieces,
1 cup

light brown sugar,
2 tablespoons firmly
packed

ground cinnamon,
¼ teaspoon

sea salt and freshly ground
pepper

granulated sugar,
1½ tablespoons, plus
1 teaspoon

granny smith apples, 3

green leaf lettuce, 1 head,
leaves torn into bite-sized
pieces

fresh goat cheese, 1 log
(9 ounces), crumbled

MAKES 6 SERVINGS

Preheat the oven to 400°F. Place the lemon halves on a small rimmed baking sheet and drizzle evenly with the 2 teaspoons olive oil. Roast until very soft, about 20 minutes. Remove from the oven and reduce the oven temperature to 350°F. When the lemon halves are cool enough to handle, squeeze ¼ cup juice and set aside.

Rinse and dry the baking sheet and line it with aluminum foil. In a bowl, whisk the egg white briefly to loosen it, and then pour off and discard half. Add the walnuts, brown sugar, cinnamon, ¼ teaspoon salt, and several grinds of pepper to the bowl with the egg white and toss to coat the nuts evenly. Spread the coated nuts evenly on the prepared baking sheet. Bake until dry and fragrant, about 20 minutes, stirring once halfway through.

As soon as the nuts are done, place the 1½ tablespoons of granulated sugar in a bowl, add the warm nuts, and toss to coat. Pour the nuts into a sieve to remove excess sugar. Let cool to room temperature.

In a small nonreactive bowl, whisk together the roasted-lemon juice, the remaining 1 teaspoon granulated sugar, ¼ teaspoon salt, and several grinds of pepper until the sugar dissolves. Slowly whisk in the ¼ cup olive oil until well blended to make a dressing. Taste and adjust the seasonings.

Quarter and core the apples, then cut them lengthwise into thin wedges.

In a large bowl, toss the lettuce with 2 pinches of salt and several grinds of pepper. Whisk the dressing to recombine, then drizzle about half of it over the lettuce and toss well (reserve the remaining dressing for another use). Taste and adjust the seasonings. Divide the dressed lettuce evenly among individual plates. Top with the apple slices and cheese, dividing them evenly, and sprinkle lightly with salt and pepper. Scatter the candied walnuts on top and serve right away.

Bitter, buttery walnuts are a classic partner to crisp apples. Here, they're candied, providing a sweet, crunchy foil to the creamy goat cheese and mildly tart dressing. Roasting lemons tempers their acidity, resulting in a mellower but more concentrated citrus flavor.

bitter greens with dried fruits and gruyère toasts

Here, honey adds a floral accent to the vinaigrette, drawing out the fruitiness of the dried apricots, figs, and cherries that top the greens. Gently bitter frisée and escarole balance the sweet elements, while Gruyère cheese, melted onto crisp baguette slices, offers its uniquely nutty and slightly sharp flavor.

Preheat the oven to 400°F.

Bring a small saucepan filled three-fourths full with water to a simmer over high heat. In a heatproof bowl, combine the apricots, figs, and cherries. Pour the simmering water over the fruit just to cover, and let stand until the fruits are softened but not mushy, 3–4 minutes. Drain and set aside.

Cut the baguette in half lengthwise, and then cut each half crosswise on the diagonal into 6 slices, each about 2½ inches wide. Arrange the slices cut side up on a rimmed baking sheet, brush the tops evenly with 3 tablespoons of the olive oil, and sprinkle lightly with salt. Bake until lightly golden and crisp, about 10 minutes. Remove from the oven and top with the Gruyère cheese, dividing it evenly. Return to the oven and bake until the cheese melts, about 5 minutes.

Meanwhile, in a small nonreactive bowl, whisk together the orange juice, vinegar, honey, shallot, ⅛ teaspoon salt, and several grinds of pepper. Slowly whisk in the remaining 2 tablespoons olive oil until well blended to make a dressing. Taste and adjust the seasonings.

In a large bowl, toss together the frisée, escarole, ¼ teaspoon salt, and several grinds of pepper. Whisk the dressing to recombine, then drizzle it over the greens and toss well. Taste and adjust the seasonings. Divide the dressed greens evenly among individual plates. Top with the softened dried fruits, dividing them evenly. Place 2 warm Gruyère cheese toasts on each plate and serve right away.

dried apricots, ½ cup packed, diced

dried mission figs, ½ cup packed, stemmed and diced

dried cherries, ½ cup packed

baguette, 1

extra-virgin olive oil, 5 tablespoons

sea salt and freshly ground pepper

gruyère cheese, ⅓ pound, shredded

fresh orange juice, ¼ cup

champagne vinegar, 2 teaspoons

honey, 1½ teaspoons

shallot, 1 small, minced

frisée, 1 small head, leaves torn into bite-sized pieces

escarole, ½ head, leaves torn into bite-sized pieces

MAKES 6 SERVINGS

Panfried oysters are unlikely salad components, but not when matched with market-fresh romaine and radicchio and finished with a creamy chive-infused dressing. The flavors are rich, yet fresh, and the crisp textures are enticing.

winter greens and fried oysters with sour cream–chive dressing

all-purpose flour, 1 cup

large eggs, 2

yellow cornmeal, 1½ cups

cayenne pepper, ¼ teaspoon

sea salt and freshly ground pepper

shucked oysters, 24, drained and picked over for shells

sour cream, ½ cup

buttermilk, ¼ cup

fresh chives, ¼ cup finely chopped

fresh lemon juice, 1½ teaspoons

dijon mustard, ½ teaspoon

sugar, ½ teaspoon

canola oil, ¼ cup

romaine lettuce, 1 small head, thinly sliced

radicchio, 1 small head, thinly sliced

MAKES 6 SERVINGS

Put the flour in a shallow bowl. In a second shallow bowl, whisk the eggs until blended. In a third shallow bowl, stir together the cornmeal, cayenne, ½ teaspoon salt, and ¼ teaspoon pepper. One at a time, dip the oysters first in the flour, coating evenly and shaking off the excess, then in the eggs, allowing the excess to drip off, and finally in the seasoned cornmeal, coating evenly and shaking off the excess. Place the coated oysters on a large plate and refrigerate for 30 minutes.

Meanwhile, in a food processor, combine the sour cream, buttermilk, chives, lemon juice, mustard, sugar, a scant ½ teaspoon salt, and several grinds of pepper and process until a creamy dressing forms, about 15 seconds. Taste and adjust the seasonings. Set aside.

Remove the coated oysters from the refrigerator and let stand at room temperature for 20 minutes. In a large sauté pan, preferably nonstick, warm the canola oil over medium-high heat until hot but not smoking. Working in batches to avoid crowding, add the oysters to the pan and cook, turning once, until golden brown and slightly crisp, about 2 minutes on each side. Using a slotted spoon, transfer to a paper towel–lined plate to drain. When all of the oysters are cooked, sprinkle them lightly with salt and tent loosely with aluminum foil to keep warm.

In a large bowl, toss together the romaine, radicchio, ¼ teaspoon salt, and several grinds of pepper. Divide the greens evenly among individual plates. Divide the fried oysters evenly among the salads and drizzle each serving with about 2 tablespoons of the dressing. Serve right away.

Here, fresh chives suffuse a tangy sour cream dressing with their sweet, onionlike flavor. The dressing's creamy coolness is the perfect foil for the cayenne pepper–laced cornmeal that coats the briny fried oysters. A bed of romaine and radicchio offers additional crunch and fresh color.

curried celery root and apple salad with golden raisins

The spiciness and golden hue of curry powder enliven this simple slaw-like salad while adding a touch of exotic flavor. Curry accentuates the earthy taste of the celery root as it complements the sweetness of both the apples and golden raisins.

Using a small, sharp knife, peel away and discard the skin from the celery root. Shred the celery root on the large holes of a box grater-shredder.

Halve and core the apples, then them cut into thin strips. Sprinkle with ½ teaspoon lemon juice to prevent them from discoloring.

In a small bowl, stir together the blanched almonds and a pinch of salt. In a large nonreactive bowl, whisk together the mayonnaise, the remaining 1½ teaspoons lemon juice, the honey, curry powder, a scant ½ teaspoon salt, and ¼ teaspoon pepper. Stir in the almonds, celery root, apples, raisins, and parsley, if using, until combined. Taste and adjust the seasonings. Transfer to a serving bowl and serve right away.

celery root, 1 (about ¾ pound)

granny smith apples, 2

fresh lemon juice, 2 teaspoons

slivered blanched almonds, 6 tablespoons, toasted (page 145)

sea salt and freshly ground pepper

mayonnaise, ½ cup plus 1½ tablespoons

honey, 1½ teaspoons

curry powder, 1⅛ teaspoons

golden raisins, 6 tablespoons

fresh flat-leaf parsley, 2 tablespoons coarsely chopped (optional)

MAKES 6 SERVINGS

warm lentil and kale salad with bacon

carrots, 6 small, peeled and cut into small dice

extra-virgin olive oil, 4 tablespoons

sea salt and freshly ground pepper

red onion, 1 large, thinly sliced

kale, 1 large bunch

garlic, 4 large cloves

fresh thyme, 10 sprigs

brown lentils, 1 cup, picked over and rinsed

chicken broth, 4 cups

bacon, 8 slices

sherry vinegar, 1 teaspoon

MAKES 6 SERVINGS

Preheat the oven to 400°F. Line a rimmed baking sheet with aluminum foil. Distribute the carrots evenly on the prepared baking sheet, drizzle with 2 tablespoons of the olive oil, sprinkle with ¾ teaspoon salt and ¼ teaspoon pepper, and toss to coat evenly. Roast until tender, about 15 minutes, stirring once or twice. Let cool to room temperature.

Meanwhile, in a nonstick frying pan over medium heat, warm the remaining 2 tablespoons olive oil. Add the onion, ¼ teaspoon salt, and several grinds of pepper and sauté until the onion is soft and lightly caramelized, about 15 minutes. Set aside.

Bring a saucepan two thirds full of water to a boil over high heat. Trim off and discard the stems from the kale, and then thinly slice the leaves. Add 1 tablespoon salt and the kale leaves to the boiling water and cook until tender, about 6 minutes. Drain in a colander. Set the saucepan aside.

Place the garlic and thyme on a square of cheesecloth, bring the corners together, and secure with kitchen string. In the same saucepan you used to cook the kale, combine the lentils, broth, ½ teaspoon salt, ¼ teaspoon pepper, and the cheesecloth sachet and bring to a boil over high heat. Reduce the heat to medium and simmer, uncovered, until the lentils are tender but not mushy, 15–20 minutes. While the lentils are cooking, in a large frying pan over medium heat, cook the bacon, turning once, until crisp and browned, about 7 minutes. Transfer to a paper towel–lined plate to drain. Let cool, and then coarsely chop.

Drain the lentils in a colander, discard the sachet, and return the lentils to the saucepan. Stir in the cooked kale, vinegar, and ½ teaspoon salt. Taste and adjust the seasonings. Transfer the lentil mixture to a serving bowl. Top with the sautéed onion, roasted carrots, and bacon. Serve right away.

Woodsy, aromatic thyme pairs beautifully with the hearty flavors of wintry ingredients. Here, it seasons brown lentils, which star in a salad that shows off myriad tastes, textures, and colors. Crisp bacon crowns the layers of lentils, roasted carrots, sautéed onions, and earthy kale.

In this eye-catching salad, boldness is the key ingredient. Tangy grapefruit is an invigorating counterpoint to the deep, distinctive taste of roasted beets. Add sharp blue cheese, bitter frisée, and licorice-scented tarragon for a surprisingly harmonious mix of flavors.

roasted beet salad with blue cheese, grapefruit, and tarragon

beets, 3 large, in assorted colors, greens removed

red grapefruits, 3 large

raspberry or red wine vinegar, 1 tablespoon

honey, 1 teaspoon

sea salt and freshly ground pepper

extra-virgin olive oil, ¼ cup

frisée, 2 heads, leaves torn into bite-sized pieces

blue cheese, such as maytag, 6 ounces, crumbled

fresh tarragon, 2½ tablespoons chopped

MAKES 6 SERVINGS

Preheat the oven to 400°F.

Wrap the beets in aluminum foil and place on a small rimmed baking sheet. Roast until tender when pierced with a sharp knife, about 1 hour and 10 minutes. Remove from the oven and unwrap. When cool enough to handle, slip off and discard the skins. Cut the beets crosswise into slices about ¼ inch thick and cut each slice into quarters.

Working with 1 grapefruit at a time, and using a thin-bladed knife, cut a thin slice off the top and bottom. Stand the fruit on a cut end, and working from top to bottom, cut away the peel and white pith in wide strips, following the contour of the fruit. Working over a bowl, slide the knife blade along both sides of each segment to free it from the membrane, capturing the segments and juice in the bowl. Repeat with the remaining grapefruits, then squeeze the membranes left behind to extract any additional juice.

Measure ⅓ cup of the grapefruit juice and place it in a small nonreactive bowl (reserve the remainder for another use). Whisk in the vinegar, honey, ¼ teaspoon salt, and several grinds of pepper. Slowly whisk in the olive oil until well blended to make a dressing. Taste and adjust the seasonings.

In a large bowl, toss the frisée with ¼ teaspoon salt and several grinds of pepper. Whisk the dressing to recombine, then drizzle about one-fourth of it over the frisée and toss well. Taste and adjust the seasonings. Divide the dressed frisée evenly among individual plates, mounding it in the center. Top each mound with grapefruit segments and beets, dividing them both evenly. Lightly season the grapefruit and beets with salt and pepper. Drizzle each salad with about 1 teaspoon of the remaining dressing (reserve the remainder for another use) and sprinkle the salads evenly with the blue cheese and tarragon. Serve right away.

Tarragon's sweet licorice flavor pairs beautifully with beets, whose earthy, sugary profile intensifies with roasting. Blue cheese adds saltiness and a rich, creamy texture that is offset by the acidity and gentle bitterness of winter's ruby grapefruit.

meyer lemon–crab salad with fresh mango

Meyer lemons, sweeter and more fragrant than traditional lemons, infuse the mayonnaise dressing for this salad with their heady citrus perfume. Creamy-textured mangoes add a tropical flair, but sweet, delicate crabmeat is the star of the show.

Finely grate the zest of 1 lemon. Halve both of the lemons and juice the halves to measure 5 tablespoons.

In a nonreactive bowl, combine the crabmeat, mayonnaise, lemon zest, 4 tablespoons of the lemon juice, ¾ teaspoon salt, and ½ teaspoon pepper and stir gently to mix. Taste and adjust the seasonings.

In a small nonreactive bowl, whisk together the remaining 1 tablespoon lemon juice, the sugar, ⅛ teaspoon salt, and several grinds of pepper until the sugar dissolves. Slowly whisk in the olive oil until well blended to make a dressing. Taste and adjust the seasonings.

Peel the mangoes and then cut the flesh into pieces about 1½ inches long and about ¼ inch thick (page 145). Don't worry if the mango pieces are uneven or irregular in shape.

In a large bowl, toss the lettuce with a pinch of salt and a few grinds of pepper. Whisk the dressing to recombine, then drizzle it over the lettuce and toss well. Taste and adjust the seasonings. Divide the dressed lettuce evenly among individual plates, arranging it in a mound in the center. Place a spoonful of the crab mixture on each mound of lettuce, dividing it evenly. Scatter the mango pieces around the crab and sprinkle with the green onions. Serve right away.

meyer lemons, 2

lump crabmeat,
1½ pounds, picked over
for shells

mayonnaise, ¾ cup

**sea salt and freshly ground
pepper**

sugar, ½ teaspoon

extra-virgin olive oil,
2 tablespoons

mangoes, 2

red leaf lettuce, 1 large
head, leaves torn into bite-
sized pieces

green onions, 4, white and
light green parts thinly
sliced

MAKES 6 SERVINGS

crisp chicken and cabbage salad with peanut dressing

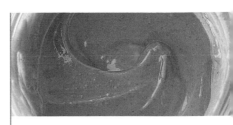

all-purpose flour, ½ cup

large egg, 1

panko **bread crumbs,** 1 cup

sea salt and freshly ground pepper

boneless, skinless chicken breast halves, 3 (about 1½ pounds total weight)

napa cabbage, 1 head

canola oil, ⅓ cup

green leaf lettuce, 12 leaves

carrots, 3 large, peeled and shredded

peanut dressing (page 144)

sesame seeds, 2 tablespoons, toasted (page 145)

MAKES 6 SERVINGS

Put the flour in a shallow bowl. In a second shallow bowl, whisk the egg until blended. In a third shallow bowl, stir together the *panko*, ½ teaspoon salt, and several grinds of pepper. Sprinkle the chicken breasts on both sides with salt and pepper. One at a time, dip the breasts first in the flour, coating evenly and shaking off the excess, then in the egg, allowing the excess to drip off, and finally in the seasoned *panko*, coating evenly and shaking off the excess. Place on a large plate and refrigerate for 30 minutes.

Pull off and discard any wilted outer leaves from the cabbage, then halve the head lengthwise and cut away the hard core from each half. Cut each half crosswise into thin slices.

Preheat the oven to 350°F. In a large nonstick frying pan over medium-high heat, warm the canola oil until hot but not smoking. Add the breaded chicken breasts and cook on the first side until golden brown, about 4 minutes. Turn and cook on the second side until golden brown, about 2 minutes longer. Transfer to a rimmed baking sheet and bake until an instant-read thermometer inserted into the thickest part of a breast registers 165°F, 15–20 minutes. Remove from the oven, sprinkle lightly with salt, and tent with aluminum foil.

In a large bowl, toss the lettuce with 2 big pinches of salt and several grinds of pepper. Line each individual plate with 2 lettuce leaves. In the same bowl, toss the cabbage and carrots with 2 big pinches of salt and several grinds of pepper. Drizzle with about one-third of the dressing and toss well.

Cut the chicken breasts crosswise into thin slices. Top the lettuce leaves with the cabbage-carrot mixture and then with the chicken slices, dividing them both evenly. Drizzle the chicken with the remaining dressing, dividing it evenly. Sprinkle with the sesame seeds and serve right away.

In this Asian-inspired recipe, the nutty, roasted taste of natural peanut butter is the backbone of the salty-sweet dressing. Sesame seeds underscore the peanut butter's earthy flavor and the toasty notes of the chicken's golden breading. The crisp and crunchy textures in this main-course salad give it enormous appeal.

Whether peppery, fruity, or buttery, extra-virgin olive oil delivers richness. Here, olive oil enhances the sweet, nutty, and herbal notes in a vegetable and fruit-studded bulgur salad, uniting the multitude of flavors and making the dish taste full, clear, and bright.

bulgur salad with roasted peppers, chickpeas, and pistachios

medium-grind bulgur wheat, 1½ cups

chicken broth, 2¼ cups

fresh lemon juice, ¼ cup

pomegranate molasses, ¼ cup

sugar, 2 teaspoons

sea salt and freshly ground pepper

extra-virgin olive oil, 6 tablespoons

chickpeas, 1 can (15½ ounces), drained and rinsed

red bell peppers, 2 large

shelled roasted pistachio nuts, ¾ cup, toasted (page 145)

fresh flat-leaf parsley, cilantro, or mint, ½ cup chopped

sweetened dried cranberries or dried sweet cherries, 1 cup

plain yogurt, 2 cups (optional)

MAKES 6 SERVINGS

Put the bulgur in a heatproof bowl. In a small saucepan over high heat, bring the broth to a boil. Pour the broth over the bulgur, cover, and let stand until the liquid has been absorbed, about 30 minutes.

Meanwhile, in a small nonreactive bowl, whisk together the lemon juice, pomegranate molasses, sugar, 1½ teaspoons salt, and several grinds of pepper until the sugar dissolves. Slowly whisk in the olive oil until well blended to make a dressing. Taste and adjust the seasonings.

In a small bowl, stir together the chickpeas and ½ teaspoon salt. Whisk the dressing to recombine, then add it, along with the chickpeas, to the bowl with the bulgur and stir to mix well. Cover and refrigerate for 2 hours.

Meanwhile, preheat the broiler. Place the bell peppers on a small rimmed baking sheet, place under the broiler, and broil, turning occasionally, until the skins are charred, about 10 minutes. Transfer to a bowl, cover, and let steam for 15 minutes. Remove and discard the skins, stems, and seeds and cut the flesh into small dice.

When ready to serve, in a small bowl, stir together the pistachios and a pinch of salt. Add the pistachios, diced peppers, parsley, and cranberries to the bulgur and toss well. Taste and adjust the seasonings. Divide the salad evenly among individual plates or bowls. Top each serving with a dollop of yogurt, if using. Serve right away.

Pomegranate molasses, a Middle Eastern specialty, has hints of fruitiness and a concentrated sweet-sour taste. Here, its intensity combines with lemon juice and olive oil to create a dressing with full-ranging flavor. Roasted peppers and dried fruits add bursts of color and sweetness, while toasted pistachios heighten the nuttiness of the bulgur wheat.

fundamentals

This section offers general advice about making great salads, as well as a handful of simple recipes that complete some of the dishes in this book. You will also find helpful tips and techniques for selecting and working with many types of fruits, vegetables, and other ingredients that are often used in the recipes.

selecting a salad

A salad can be many things. It can be a simple mixture of lettuce leaves tossed with an oil and vinegar dressing; it can be an elaborate composition of greens, fruits, nuts, and cheese; or it can be a medley of vegetables and tender cooked grains without a single leafy green in sight. A salad can be served as a first course or appetizer; as a hearty main dish for a luncheon or supper; as a side dish or accompaniment to a meal; or, as in some European traditions, it can be a palate refresher that follows the main course.

When deciding what kind of salad to make, first think about what is in season and try to take advantage of locally grown ingredients because they're sure to taste better than produce shipped in from afar. Then, consider at which point during the meal you would like to serve a salad. For instance, as a first course or appetizer, a leafy green salad with multiple components, such as Apple Salad with Candied Walnuts and Roasted-Lemon Dressing (page 119), is appropriate because

without the distraction of a main dish, the salad's complexity can be fully appreciated. But for a side dish to a casual family meal, a chunky home-style salad, such as Potato and Green Bean Salad with Herbs and Anchovies (page 70), is ideal. Finally, choose a salad with flavors that fit nicely into your menu. For example, Jicama-Mango Salad with Cilantro Dressing (page 24) would be perfect for a Mexican-themed dinner, while Broccoli and Cauliflower Salad with Pickled Onions and Bacon (page 98) would be well suited to a cookout or picnic.

washing and drying greens

At the grocery store, heads and bunches of lettuce and greens are often sprayed with water to keep them fresh and perky. Once in a plastic bag and in your refrigerator, however, the moisture they've collected has a deleterious effect: It hastens spoilage. At farmers' markets, produce is usually not subjected to the same wet treatment, but locally and organically grown greens are often very gritty and sandy between their layers of leaves. No matter

where you purchase your salad greens, it's best to tend to them immediately after you bring them home.

One of the best ways to wash greens is to fill a clean kitchen sink or a large bowl with cool water. Gently pull the leaves off the head or trim the bottom of the bunch to separate the stems. Discard any bruised, wilted, or discolored leaves. Submerge the greens in the water and gently swish them about to loosen any dirt. Let the greens stand for a few minutes to allow the grit to settle to the bottom, then lift the greens out of the water, transferring them to a large colander or clean kitchen towel. Dry them, in batches if necessary, in a salad spinner or loosely enclose them in the kitchen towel and gently shake and toss them until they are as dry as can be.

storing greens

in a salad spinner If you have the room in your refrigerator, a salad spinner is a good place to store washed and dried greens because it allows the greens to breathe, all the while creating a humid environment that prevents them from drying out. In addition, a salad spinner protects delicate greens from being crushed by other items in the refrigerator.

in a kitchen towel If you don't have a salad spinner, lay out a clean kitchen towel and spread the washed greens on it, roughly in a single layer. Very gently and loosely roll up the towel with the greens in it, like a jelly roll, taking care not to crush them. Place the roll in a large plastic bag or carefully wrap it in plastic wrap and refrigerate.

making oil-based dressings

with a whisk The classic method for making an oil-based salad dressing is with a whisk. The acidic component, usually either vinegar or fruit juice, is added to a bowl along with salt, pepper, and sometimes sugar. The oil is added gradually while the mixture is whisked constantly. This process helps to form a well-blended dressing, a stable emulsion that will eventually separate, but will do so slowly. If the dressing separates upon standing, be sure to whisk it to recombine before use.

in a jar A very simple, no-fuss method of making an oil-based salad dressing is to simply add the dressing ingredients all at once to a small glass jar with a tight-fitting lid. Seal the jar and shake vigorously until a blended dressing forms. The downside to this technique is that it yields a weaker emulsion, which means that the dressing will separate more quickly than if made by whisking. If it separates upon standing, be sure to shake it again before use.

seasoning salads

For the best-tasting salads, it's important that each component be seasoned before the dish is assembled. After making a dressing,

taste it and adjust the salt and pepper, keeping in mind that assertive seasoning is desirable. Seasoning the greens, other vegetables, fruits, and garnishes, such as nuts, separately before assembly may seem fussy, but these extra steps heighten the flavors of the individual ingredients, so when put together, the salad tastes full and complex.

dressing salads

Before dressing greens to make a salad, be sure that the greens are as dry as possible. Excess residual water clinging to the leaves will dilute the dressing, making the salad taste weak and watery.

Place the greens in a bowl that seems oversized for the amount—having room makes tossing easy. If you're using an oil-based dressing and if it has separated upon standing, whisk it well to recombine. Drizzle—do not pour—the dressing over the greens in the bowl so that they do not become drenched or soggy. With a pair of salad servers or tongs, or even your hands, gently toss and fluff the greens, using a very light touch, until they are evenly coated. Be sure to reach down into the bottom of the bowl where the dresssing, especially one with a thin texture, collects.

The recipes in this book recommend using specific amounts of dressing. However, if you prefer your salads lightly dressed, you should start with a slightly smaller amount and add more if you deem it necessary. If you prefer

your salad generously coated with dressing, begin with the recommended amount, taste the dressed greens, and add more dressing to suit your taste.

In general, once dressed, greens do not keep well, so dress only as much as you intend to serve and store the unused greens and dressing separately.

mixing and matching greens and dressings

This book is filled with ideas for complete salads—recipes match salad components with dressings and garnishes to create delicious dishes with complementary and contrasting elements. Feel free, however, to mix and match salad components to create inspired salads that bear your signature.

When designing your own creations, keep in mind that delicate greens, such as mesclun and mâche, are best suited to light, oil-based dressings. Sturdy greens, such as romaine lettuce, butter lettuce, and cabbage, can stand up to rich, creamy dressings. Try to balance tangy, spicy, and bitter tastes with mild and mellow flavors when assembling components. Think about pairing crisp, crunchy textures with tender, yielding ones and sweet ingredients with savory accents. With a bounty of vegetables, fruits, cheeses, nuts, herbs, and grains available to us, there is no limit to creating wonderful salads.

lemongrass-mint paste

2 stalks lemongrass

½ cup chopped fresh mint

2 tablespoons fresh lime juice

2 tablespoons canola oil

1 teaspoon minced jalapeño chile

2 cloves garlic, minced

¼ teaspoon sea salt

⅛ teaspoon freshly ground pepper

Using a chef's knife, cut off the tops of the lemongrass stalks where they begin to toughen and discard them, then trim off the hard, fibrous bottoms. Pull off and discard the dry outer layers of the stalks to reveal the tender pale green interiors. Thinly slice the stalks crosswise.

Transfer the sliced lemongrass to a food processor and process until finely chopped, about 10 seconds. Add the mint, lime juice, canola oil, chile, garlic, salt, and pepper and process until a paste forms, about 10 seconds. Makes about ¾ cup.

smoked paprika marinade

½ cup extra-virgin olive oil

⅓ cup sherry vinegar

2 tablespoons fresh orange juice

1 tablespoon spanish sweet smoked paprika

5 cloves garlic, minced

1½ tablespoons fresh oregano leaves

In a nonreactive bowl, stir together the olive oil, vinegar, orange juice, paprika, garlic, and oregano until blended. Makes about 1 cup.

olive-anchovy vinaigrette

2 tablespoons chopped pitted niçoise olives

2 or 3 olive oil–packed anchovy fillets

5 tablespoons extra-virgin olive oil

3 tablespoons white wine vinegar

2 tablespoons finely chopped fresh chives

¾ teaspoon sugar

¼ teaspoon dijon mustard

In a food processor, combine the olives and anchovies and process until smooth, about 10 seconds. Add the olive oil, vinegar, chives, sugar, and mustard and process until a smooth dressing forms, about 10 seconds. Makes about ¾ cup.

peanut dressing

¼ cup creamy natural peanut butter

¼ cup rice vinegar

¼ cup canola oil

1 tablespoon sesame oil

2 tablespoons brown sugar, firmly packed

1 teaspoon reduced-sodium tamari

¾ teaspoon sea salt

In a food processor or blender, combine the peanut butter, vinegar, canola oil, sesame oil,

brown sugar, tamari, salt, and 2 tablespoons water and process until a smooth dressing forms, about 15 seconds. Taste and adjust the seasonings. Makes about ¾ cup.

balsamic syrup

1 cup balsamic vinegar

Bring the balsamic vinegar to a boil in a small nonreactive saucepan over high heat and cook until thick, syrupy, and reduced to about ¼ cup, 10–12 minutes. Let cool to room temperature. Makes about ¼ cup.

hard-cooked eggs

6 large eggs

Place the eggs in a saucepan, add cold water to cover by 2 inches, and bring to a boil over medium heat.

When the water begins to boil, remove the saucepan from the heat, cover, and let stand for 20 minutes. Uncover and rinse the eggs under cold running water until cool. Makes 6 hard-cooked eggs.

poached eggs

1 tablespoon distilled white vinegar

1 teaspoon sea salt

6 large eggs

Pour water to a depth of at least 1½ inches into a large frying pan. Add the vinegar and bring to a vigorous simmer over medium-high heat. Reduce the heat to medium or medium-low so that water simmers gently.

Meanwhile, fill a large, wide bowl two-thirds full with ice water, stir in the salt, and place near the stove top. Crack 1 egg into each of 6 ramekins or other small heatproof cups. When the water is ready, holding a ramekin near the edge of the pan, gently slide the egg into the simmering water. Repeat with the remaining eggs.

Poach the eggs until the whites are firm and opaque but the yolks are still soft, 2–3 minutes. Using a slotted spoon, transfer the poached eggs to the ice water and let stand for 1 minute. Using the slotted spoon, scoop the eggs one at a time from the ice water, trim the egg whites with kitchen scissors to make neat edges, and set aside on a plate at room temperature for up to 1 hour. Makes 6 poached eggs.

toasting nuts and seeds

Toasting nuts and seeds crisps their texture and lightly browns them, giving them a rich, full flavor. Be sure to let toasted nuts and seeds cool to room temperature before use.

in the oven Scatter the nuts or seeds in an even layer in a baking dish or on a rimmed baking sheet. Toast in a 325°F to 350°F oven, stirring once or twice, until fragrant and slightly darkened in color, 5–10 minutes, depending on the size and quantity of the nuts or seeds.

on the stove top Place the nuts or seeds in an even layer in a frying pan. Toast over medium heat, stirring or shaking the pan often, until fragrant and slightly darkened in color, 2–5 minutes, depending on the size and quantity of the nuts or seeds.

hulling strawberries

Hull fresh strawberries after washing them and just before use.

1 Insert the tip of a paring knife Insert the tip of a sharp paring knife at a slight angle just below the stem area until the tip of the knife reaches the center of the berry.

2 Trim and pull off the top Cut around the stem area, rotating the berry to make a circular cut. Gently pull or pry off the top.

working with mangoes

Look for mangoes that feel heavy for their size. They should be fragrant and the flesh should give to gentle pressure. If the fruit is underripe, let it ripen at room temperature for a couple days before use.

1 Peel the mango Using a sharp vegetable peeler, remove the skin from the mango.

2 Cut off the top Using a chef's knife or utility knife, cut off a thin slice from the stem end of the fruit.

3 Cut the flesh from the pit Stand the mango on the cut side. Cut down the length of the fruit along one of its flat sides, about ½ inch off the center, just grazing the flat central pit. Repeat on the second flat side of the mango. As best you can, trim away the flesh that is clinging to the pit in large pieces.

4 Cut the flesh into smaller pieces Dice or cut the flesh as called for in the recipe.

working with pineapple

When shopping for pineapple, select one that feels heavy for its size with vibrant green leaves. It should also have a fruity fragrance—an indication that the fruit is ripe—and be free of bruises and blemishes. To remove its thick, scaly skin, follow these steps:

1 Cut off the top and bottom Using a sharp chef's knife, cut off the top and bottom of the fruit and stand it upright on a cut side.

2 Slice off the skin Working from top to bottom, slice off the skin in wide strips. Cut deep enough to remove most of the brown "eyes," but not too much of the flesh.

3 Cut out the eyes Using the tip of a paring knife, remove any remaining eyes.

peeling avocados

Avocados arrive in markets when they are still quite firm and underripe. When buying, look for ones that have at least some give to their flesh, then let them ripen at room temperature for a few days until they yield to gentle pressure.

1 Cut the avocado in half Using a chef's knife, cut the avocado in half lengthwise, cutting down to and around the pit.

2 Separate the halves Hold the avocado so that one of the halves rests in each hand. Gently rotate the halves in opposite directions to separate them.

3 Remove the pit Carefully holding the half with the pit in one hand, strike the pit with the heel of the knife blade, lodging it in the pit. Twist the knife and pull out the pit.

4 Peel the avocado Carefully peel off the thick skin, using a paring knife as needed to help separate the skin from the flesh so that it can be easily peeled away.

working with citrus

Citrus zest and juice are often used in salads to add bright fragrance and flavor.

zesting If a recipe calls for both citrus zest and juice, zest the fruit before juicing because it is easier to zest when it is whole. To grate citrus zest, use a fine-toothed rasp-style grater. Using light pressure, move the fruit back and forth against the grater's teeth, removing only the colored rind and leaving behind the white pith, which is bitter tasting. For large strips, use a sharp vegetable peeler to remove the zest in long, wide pieces, working from pole to pole.

juicing To get the most juice from a citrus fruit, it helps if the fruit is at room temperature. Just

before juicing, roll it back and forth along a work surface under the palm of your hand, applying firm pressure so that the fruit softens slightly. Cut the fruit in half crosswise, then use a citrus press or reamer to squeeze the juice from each half. Pour the squeezed juice into a fine-mesh sieve set over a bowl or measuring cup to remove any bits of pulp and seeds.

slicing fennel

When shopping for fennel, look for firm, blemish-free bulbs with vibrant green fronds.

1 Trim the stalks Using a chef's knife, trim off the stalks. If desired, set the fronds aside to use as garnish.

2 Remove any discolored parts Run a sharp vegetable peeler over the outer layer of the bulb to remove any tough or discolored areas. If the outer layer is badly bruised, remove it entirely and discard.

3 Quarter the bulb Using the chef's knife, cut the bulb lengthwise into quarters, cutting right through the bulb's core.

4 Cut away the core Cut away the tough core from each quarter.

5 Slice each quarter Cut each quarter into slices either lengthwise or crosswise.

mincing shallots

Shallots add a mellow onion- and garlic-like flavor to many types of salad dressings. When

mincing shallots for a dressing, make sure that the pieces are very fine so that their texture is minimized.

1 Halve the shallot Using a sharp paring knife, halve the shallot lengthwise through the root end, then trim off and discard the sprout end from each half.

2 Peel away the skin Use the knife blade to help peel back the papery skin, then pull off the skin from each half.

3 Make a series of lengthwise cuts Set one half cut side down on a cutting board. Make a series of lengthwise cuts spaced very close together. Do not cut through the root end; it helps to hold the shallot layers together.

4 Make a series of horizontal cuts Position the root end of the shallot half to the left if you are right-handed or to the right if you are left-handed. With the knife blade held parallel with the board, make a series of horizontal cuts starting at the sprout end and stopping short of the root end.

5 Make a series of crosswise cuts Starting from the sprout end and working toward the root end of the shallot half, make a series of crosswise cuts spaced very close together to yield mince. Repeat steps 3 through 5 with the remaining shallot half.

mincing fresh chiles

When working with chiles, it's a good idea to wear rubber gloves to protect your hands from the chiles' heat. If you don't wear gloves, be sure to thoroughly wash your hands when you're done working with the chiles.

1 *Quarter the chile lengthwise* Using a sharp paring knife, trim off and discard the stem end of the chile. Quarter the chile lengthwise.

2 *Remove the seeds and ribs* Using the paring knife, trim away the seeds and ribs from the inside of each chile quarter.

3 *Slice the quarters into strips* Using a sharp chef's knife, cut each quarter lengthwise into very thin strips.

4 *Mince the strips* Line up the chile strips into a bundle and cut them crosswise into very fine pieces. If necessary, to mince even finer, gather the pieces and rock the knife blade back and forth over them until they are of the desired fineness.

pitting olives

Some types of olives are sold already pitted, but many specialty olives, including the oil-cured and Niçoise olives used in this book, are usually sold with their pits. One way to remove their pits is with an olive pitter, but a meat pounder or chef's knife works too.

1 *Crush the olives* Place the olives in a zipper-lock plastic bag, force out the air, and seal closed. Using a meat pounder or rolling pin, gently crush the olives until the flesh splits open. Alternatively, press on the olives with the flat side of a chef's knife.

2 *Remove the pits* Remove the crushed olives from the bag and separate the pits from the olive flesh with your fingers. Use a paring knife to cut the flesh from the pits of any stubborn olives.

removing pin bones from salmon fillets

Before cooking fish fillets, be sure to check for and remove any tiny pin bones that may be concealed within the flesh.

1 *Feel for any pin bones* Lay a fish fillet skin (or skinned) side down on the work surface. Run a fingertip along the center of the fillet. If you feel the tips of tiny bones sticking up, the pin bones are still in place and should be removed before cooking.

2 *Pull out the pin bones* Using fish tweezers or needle-nose pliers, pull out the bones one by one, gripping the tip of each one and pulling up and out on a slight diagonal with the grain of the flesh.

preparing a charcoal grill

On the fire bed of a charcoal grill, ignite about 2½ pounds of coals in a large chimney starter and let the coals burn until covered with a thin coating of white ash.

direct-heat cooking over high heat Empty the coals into the fire bed, then arrange them in an even pile over one half of the fire bed, leaving the other half free of coals. Replace the grill grate and brush it lightly with oil to prevent food from sticking. When cooking, use the side of the grill with coals.

direct heat cooking over medium-high heat Empty the coals into the fire bed, then spread them into an even layer on the fire bed and let burn until medium-hot, 20–30 minutes. Replace the grill grate and brush it lightly with oil to prevent food from sticking.

preparing a gas grill

Before using a propane grill, be sure that there is enough fuel in the tank. Open the grill cover, ignite the grill, and turn all the burners to high heat. Close the cover and preheat the grill for 10–20 minutes.

direct-heat cooking over high heat Open the grill cover and leave the burners on high. Lightly brush the grill grate with oil to prevent food from sticking.

direct-heat cooking over medium-high heat Open the grill cover, then reduce the burners to medium-high heat. Lightly brush the grill grate with oil to prevent food from sticking.

seasonal ingredients

Fresh fruits and vegetables taste best when they are at the height of their season. The chart at right indicates the seasonality of most types of produce used in this book. Note that though some items are available throughout the year, they do have seasons when they are particularly flavorful. In addition, keep in mind that seasonality often varies with different growing regions. Solid dots mark peak seasons; open dots indicate transitional ones.

INGREDIENTS	SPRING	SUMMER	FALL	WINTER
apples			●	○
artichokes, baby	●		●	
asian pears			●	●
asparagus	●			
beans, fava	●			
beans, green		●		
beets	●	●	●	●
bell peppers		●	●	
broccoli		●	●	●
butternut squash			●	●
cauliflower		●	●	●
celery		●	●	○
celery root			●	○
chiles, fresh		●	●	
corn, sweet		●		
cucumbers		●		
eggplant		●	○	
fennel	●	●	●	●
figs		●	○	
grapefruit	○			●
grapes			●	●

INGREDIENTS	SPRING	SUMMER	FALL	WINTER
haricots verts		●		
jicama	●	●	●	●
kale			●	●
mangoes	●	●	●	●
meyer lemons	○			●
mushrooms, wild			●	●
onions, vidalia	●			
oranges	●	●	●	●
parsnips	○		●	●
peaches		●		
pears			●	●
pineapple	●	●	●	●
pomelo			●	●
potatoes	●	●	●	●
potatoes, new	●			
radishes	●	●	●	
raspberries	●	●		
strawberries	●	●		
tomatoes		●	○	
watermelon		●		
zucchini		●	○	

glossary

anchovy fillets, oil-packed Harvested in waters worldwide, these small silver fish are popular in the Mediterranean. Oil-packed anchovy fillets are sold in tins and jars.

artichokes, baby The flower buds from a plant belonging to the thistle family, artichokes are prized for their slightly nutty flavor and succulent, buttery texture. Contrary to what their name suggests, baby artichokes are not immature artichokes, but rather the small flower buds that grow lower down on the plant. Baby artichokes lack the fuzzy choke that must be removed from the center of large artichokes.

Asian pears There are many varieties of these fruits that are popular throughout China, Japan, and Korea. Resembling a cross between apples and traditional pears, they range widely in color and size, but a juicy, crisp, slightly granular texture is characteristic of all types of Asian pears.

beans, fava Also called broad beans, this springtime bean has an earthy, slightly bitter flavor. The edible portion must be removed from the large outer pod, and then each bean must be slipped out of its tough skin.

bulgur wheat Nutty-tasting bulgur is made by steaming wheat, partly removing the bran, and then drying and cracking the grains. Sold in fine, medium, and coarse grinds, it has a mild flavor and firm texture that make it a good vehicle for the flavors of other ingredients. Look for it in well-stocked grocery stores, Middle Eastern markets, and natural foods stores where it is sometimes sold in bulk.

cabbage, napa Also called Chinese cabbage or celery cabbage, this elongated variety has wrinkly, light yellow-green leaves and a crisp-textured pearly white core.

capers Flower buds from a shrub native to the Mediterranean, capers are usually sold pickled in a vinegar brine. Those labeled "nonpareils," from the south of France, are the smallest and considered the best.

celery root Also known as celeriac, celery root is a knobby, round fall and winter vegetable that contributes a subtle celery flavor when cooked and a crisp crunch to salads when used raw.

cheeses Cheese adds unique flavor and texture to many dishes, including salads. To ensure freshness, purchase cheese from a specialty cheese shop.

blue Blue cheeses have been treated with mold and have formed bluish veins or pockets of mold that give the cheese its strong, piquant flavor. They range in texture from dry and crumbly to soft and creamy.

bocconcini From the Italian word meaning "morsel," bocconcini are small rounds of fresh mozzarella cheese. They are sold packed in whey in well-stocked markets and specialty cheese shops.

dry Jack This California cheese is made from cow's milk. The cheese is cured, rubbed with oil, cocoa, and pepper, and aged for up to 10 months, giving its rind its characteristic dark color. The flavor of dry Jack is rich and nutty, and its hard, dry texture makes the cheese well suited to grating and shaving.

goat, fresh Also called chèvre, this pure white cheese is made from goat's milk and has a soft texture and a pleasantly tangy, slightly salty flavor. Do not use aged goat cheese in a recipe calling for fresh.

Gouda, aged This cow's-milk cheese hails from Holland. Young Gouda has a semifirm texture and mild flavor, but when aged, it becomes dry and hard and its flavor takes on a pleasantly sharp nuttiness and a full, rich taste with hints of caramel.

Gruyère A firm, nutty-tasting cow's-milk cheese, Gruyère is a Swiss cheese named for the alpine region in which it originated. It is also produced in France, where it is called Gruyère de Comté, or simply Comté. Both types have smooth melting qualities.

feta A white, crumbly sheep's- or cow's-milk cheese that is cured in brine, feta is a traditional Greek cheese, though it is now made in many countries, including the United States and France. It has a salty, tangy flavor.

Parmigiano-Reggiano This true Parmesan cheese is made from cow's milk in northern Italy according to strict standards. Versions made in other countries are also available, but none can match the rich, nutty, and complex flavor of Parmigiano-Reggiano.

pecorino romano An Italian sheep's-milk cheese made around Rome, pecorino romano has a sharp, salty, and peppery flavor. Its firm, grainy texture is good for grating.

provolone A semifirm Italian cheese made from cow's milk, provolone has a smooth, dense texture. Young provolone is mild and creamy in flavor; aged provolone is drier and has a sharper taste.

ricotta salata A variation on ricotta cheese, ricotta salata has a firm, dry texture and a salty and milky flavor. It can be crumbled or grated onto dishes.

chickpeas Also known as garbanzo beans or *ceci* beans, these rich, nutty-flavored beans are beige in color, round in shape, and have a firm texture.

chiles When buying fresh chiles, seek out ones that are plump, firm, and blemish free.

chipotle chiles in adobo sauce Chipotle chiles are ripe red jalapeños that have been smoked and dried. To make chipotle chiles in adobo sauce, the dried chiles are packed in a vinegary seasoned tomato sauce. They are sold canned in most supermarkets.

jalapeño This green chile, averaging about 2 inches in length, ranges from hot to very hot and is one of the most widely used chiles in the United States.

poblano Deep green with broad shoulders and a tapered body, a poblano chile is about 5 inches long. It is only mildly hot and has a green, earthy flavor. Poblano chiles that are dried are known as ancho chiles.

chili powder This spice blend combines dried chiles, cumin, oregano, garlic, and other spices. It is often used in the cooking of the American Southwest but is never used in authentic Mexican cooking. Do not mistake chili powder with pure ground chile powder, which is simply dried chile pods ground into a fine powder.

cornichons From the French meaning "little horns," cornichons are tiny gherkin pickles with a briny, tangy flavor. They are used to add zest to sauces and are a traditional accompaniment to pâté.

couscous, Israeli Sometimes called pearl couscous, Israeli couscous is pasta shaped into small pellets that are larger than the more common and very finely textured regular North African couscous. It is sold in most Middle Eastern markets and well-stocked grocery stores.

crabmeat, lump Crabmeat taken from the meaty portion near the center of the crab is sold as lump crabmeat. The pieces are large, white, and delicately flavored. It is often sold packed in small tubs in fish markets and in the refrigerated seafood section of well-stocked grocery stores.

crème fraîche In the French tradition, crème fraîche is unpasteurized cream thickened by bacteria that is naturally present in the cream. More commonly, though, it is cream thickened by a bacteria that is added, yielding a soft, spreadable consistency and a tangy, slightly nutty flavor.

crystallized ginger Sometimes called candied ginger, crystallized ginger is made by cooking fresh ginger in a sugar syrup and then coating it with coarse sugar crystals. It is usually sold in thin slices.

cucumber, English Slender, dark green English cucumbers, also called hothouse or hydroponic cucumbers, have thinner skins and fewer seeds than regular cucumbers. They are often sold shrink-wrapped in plastic alongside regular cucumbers.

curry powder Curry powder is a convenience product meant to simplify the daily chore of blending spices for Indian cooks. It is a complex mixture of ground chiles, spices, seeds, and herbs.

edamame Green soybeans often go by their Japanese name, edamame. They are sold frozen, both in their pods and shelled.

endive, Belgian A member of the chicory family, Belgian endive is grown using a labor-intensive method that forces the roots to sprout in a dark environment. The result is tightly furled conical shoots with a creamy white color, from the lack of chlorophyll, and just a touch of yellowish green at the edges and tips. Belgian endive has a pleasantly bitter flavor and can be used in cooked and raw preparations.

escarole The robust, slightly curled leaves of this chicory relative are slightly bitter, but pleasantly so. Delicious raw, the sturdy leaves of escarole can also stand up to light cooking or warm dressings.

farro This variety of wheat is also sometimes known as emmer. It is considered to have ancient origins and was, at one time, popular in Mediterranean and Middle Eastern cuisines. Today, it is used most notably in Italian cooking. The wholesome grain's cooked texture is quite chewy, and its flavor nutty.

fish sauce, Asian Made from salted and fermented fish, fish sauce is a thin, clear liquid that ranges in color from amber to dark brown. Southeast Asians use it in the same way Westerners use salt, both as a cooking ingredient and as a seasoning at the table.

frisée Also called curly endive, this member of the chicory family is pale yellow-green, with thin, spiraling fringed leaves and a refreshingly bitter taste. At its best during the cold months, it is typically combined in small amounts with other mild greens to provide a contrast in color, flavor, and texture.

haricots verts Also known as French green beans, haricots verts are small, slender beans favored in France. They are more tender in texture and more delicately flavored than regular green beans.

harissa This fiery North African spice paste is used both as a seasoning and as a condiment. It is made with chiles, spices, garlic, and olive oil and is sold in tubes, cans, and jars. Look for it in well-stocked grocery stores and Middle Eastern markets.

hoisin sauce A thick, brown, salty-sweet sauce, hoisin sauce is used both as an ingredient and as a condiment in Chinese cooking. It is made with soybeans, garlic, vinegar, chiles, and other flavorful spices.

jicama A round tuber with a mild, sweet flavor and very crunchy texture, this root vegetable can be eaten raw or cooked. Before use, its golden beige skin must be peeled away to reveal its white flesh. Choose a thin-skinned jicama that feels heavy for its size.

lemongrass This herb with a fresh lemon flavor, but with none of lemon's brassiness, resembles a green onion with pale gray-green leaves. The tender inner core contains the most flavor. Lemongrass is a common flavoring in Southeast Asian cooking.

lettuces The array of lettuces available in grocery stores and farmers' markets provides year-round variety for the salad bowl.

butter Sometimes called Boston lettuce, butter lettuce grows in loose heads. The light green and slightly ruffled leaves are tender in texture and mild in flavor.

green leaf Heads of this all-purpose salad green are formed of large, ruffled, loosely packed leaves. Their texture is tender and their flavor is very mild and delicate .

red leaf This lettuce shares the qualities of green leaf lettuce but has a deep red blush on the leaf edges and tops.

romaine Romaine lettuce grows in elongated heads, with crisp, sturdy leaves that have hints of sweetness. It holds up well to assertive dressings and garnishes.

mâche Also known as lamb's lettuce, field salad, and corn salad, mâche is a salad green with a tender texture and slightly nutty flavor. The small, dark green leaves are very delicate and tend to bruise easily, so mâche is best used within a day or two of purchase. Look for it in well-stocked grocery stores.

mesclun From the Provençal word for "mix," this colorful salad medley contains a variety of young, tender salad greens, often including arugula, frisée, oakleaf lettuce, spinach, and radicchio. Mesclun is frequently sold in bags, and sometimes loose in bulk.

Meyer lemon Believed to be a cross between a regular lemon and a mandarin orange, Meyer lemons typically have thin skins and turn a deep orangish yellow color when ripe. Their fragrant juice and flesh are sweeter and less acidic than regular lemons.

mustards A popular condiment with bold, tangy taste, mustard not only adds flavor to salad dressings, it helps to keep a vinaigrette or dressing emulsified, or well blended, slowing the rate at which the oil and vinegar (or other liquid) separate.

Dijon Silky smooth and sharp and peppery, this mustard originates in Dijon, France. It is made with brown or black mustard seeds and white wine.

whole-grain This type of mustard has a rustic, speckled appearance and a coarse texture because it is made with whole, not ground, mustard seeds.

nonreactive Untreated aluminum or cast iron pans can react with acidic ingredients such as citrus juice, vinegar, or wine, giving them a metallic flavor and an off color. When in doubt, choose stainless steel, anodized aluminum, or enameled cast iron pans for cooking and stainless steel, glass, or ceramic bowls for mixing acidic ingredients.

nuts Nuts add texture, richness, and color to salads. For use in cooking, look for unsalted nuts so that you can control the amount of seasoning that goes into the dish. Storing nuts in an airtight container in the freezer or refrigerator helps keep them fresh.

almonds The meat found inside the pit of a fruit related to peaches, the almond is mildly sweet and fragrant with a firm, pleasantly crunchy texture.

almonds, Marcona These round, flat almonds are a Spanish specialty. They are usually sold fried or roasted, which brings out a sweet, rich, toasty flavor.

cashews These smooth, kidney-shaped nuts, from a tree that is native to Africa and India, are always sold removed from their hard shell. They have a sweet, buttery flavor.

peanuts Actually a type of legume, peanuts are seeds that grow underground in waffle-veined pods. When roasted, their earthy flavor becomes full and toasty and their texture firm, with a slight starchiness.

pecans A native of North America, the pecan has two deeply furrowed lobes housed in a smooth brown oval-shaped shell. Pecans' sweet flavor contains notes of caramel, butterscotch, and smoke.

pine nuts The seeds of pine trees, pine nuts have thin, deep brown shells and grow nestled inside of pine cones. Most often they are sold shelled. They boast a rich, soft texture and woodsy, resinous flavor.

pistachios Pistachios, light green kernels encased in hard, tan-colored shells, are widely used in Mediterranean, Middle Eastern, and Indian cuisines. Their nutty flavor is rather delicate. They are sold both in their shells and shelled; for cooking, look for the latter and avoid bright red pistachios that owe their color to vegetable dye.

walnuts A relative of the pecan, walnuts have a buttery texture. Their flavor is rich, with an assertive, but pleasant bitterness.

oils There is a wide variety of oils available to cooks today. Some types are best used for high-heat cooking, some for drizzling over a finished dish as a flavor accent, and some for use in salad dressings.

canola This neutral-tasting oil is pressed from rapeseed, a relative of the mustard plant. High in monounsaturated fat, it is good for general cooking. It also has a high smoking point and can be used for frying.

extra-virgin olive The first cold pressing of olives yields extra-virgin olive oil, the variety that is the lowest in acid and the purest, with a full, rich flavor that reflects where the olives were grown.

sesame Sesame oil, pressed from white sesame seeds, is light in color and mildly nutty in flavor. Do not mistake it for Asian sesame oil that is made from toasted sesame seeds and has a dark color and distinctive, assertive flavor.

walnut Pressed from walnut meats, walnut oil has a rich, nutty flavor and fragrance. It is not used for cooking because its flavor is lost when heated; it is often used in salad dressings or for drizzling onto finished dishes.

olives A Mediterranean staple, olives add both color and bold flavor to salads.

niçoise These small black olives are named for the city of Nice in France's Provence region. Niçoise olives are not very fleshy, but they have a rich, meaty, and relatively mellow olive flavor.

oil-cured Oil-cured olives are small, dry, and have a wrinkly, shriveled appearance. Their flavor is pleasantly bitter and their texture is silky and rich.

onions, Vidalia These thin-skinned onions take their name from Vidalia, Georgia, where they are grown. They are juicy, sweet, and available in the spring. When not in season, other sweet onions are good subtitutes.

orzo The Italian word for "barley," this pasta shape resembles large, flat grains of rice. It is particulary well suited for use in soup and salad preparations.

pancetta Pancetta is unsmoked Italian bacon. To make it, pork belly is salted and seasoned with black pepper and other spices before it is rolled into a cylinder and cured. It gives meaty flavor to soups, braises, pasta sauces, salads, and dishes of all kinds.

panko These Japanese bread crumbs have a coarse, but very light and airy, texture. Look for *panko* in well-stocked grocery stores and Asian markets.

paprika, Spanish sweet smoked A Spanish specialty, smoked paprika is made from red chiles that have been smoked and then ground. It has a very earthy, smoky, and almost meaty flavor and a deep red color. Smoked paprika is available in sweet or mild (dulce), bittersweet (agridulce), and hot (picante) varieties.

peperoncini These pickled, mildly spicy yellow-green chiles are packed in brine and sold in jars. In Italy, however, peperoncini are red chiles, and the word is used to refer to the fresh, dried, and pickled forms.

piquillo peppers *Piquillos* are a specialty of Northern Spain and are popular in Basque cuisine. They are hand picked, fire roasted, and peeled prior to being packed in water or oil in jars or cans.

pomegranate molasses This thick, deep red, sweet-tart syrup is pomegranate juice that has been reduced to a strong concentrate. It is sold in bottles in Middle Eastern markets and well-stocked supermarkets.

pomelo The largest of the citrus fruits, pomelo is native to Southeast Asia. It resembles grapefruit, but lacks grapefruit's bitter quality. Pomelo's thick, spongy rind conceals pale yellow to pink colored flesh that can be extremely juicy or very dry, with a flavor that is sweet but tangy.

Port, ruby True Port, a sweet fortified wine with jammy, concentrated flavors, hails from Portugal. There are several different varieties of Port; ruby Port has a fiery quality and is the least expensive type, making it a good choice for cooking.

prosciutto True Italian-made prosciutto from the Emilia-Romagna region, called prosciutto di Parma, is the seasoned, salt-cured, air-dried rear leg of pork. Aged from 10 months to 2 years, prosciutto di Parma is considered the best, and its production is overseen by a governing consortium.

pumpkin seeds, shelled Also called *pepitas*, shelled pumpkin seeds are green in color and have a slightly vegetal and nutty flavor.

quinoa A staple of the ancient Incas of Peru, this highly nutritious grain looks like spherical sesame seeds. When cooked, quinoa has a mild taste and light, fluffy texture. It must be rinsed well before cooking because the grain has a natural residue that is very bitter tasting.

radicchio A red-leafed chicory, radicchio has a bitter flavor and a tender but firm texture. Radicchio di Verona and radicchio di Treviso are the two common varieties; the former is globe shaped and the latter is narrow and tapered like Belgian endive.

Sriracha sauce The bright red-orange sauce is a mixture of ground chiles, tomatoes, vinegar, garlic, salt, and sugar. Originating in Sriracha in southern Thailand, this general-purpose sauce is used sparingly to add zest to a wide range of cooked dishes. It is also used as a table condiment for many Southeast Asian dishes.

tamari, reduced-sodium Regular soy sauce is made from fermented soybeans and wheat. Tamari is a type of soy sauce made without the addtion of wheat. It has a full body and intense flavor. Reduced-sodium tamari allows the cook to better control the amount of salt that goes into the dish in which it is used.

tuna Tuna comes from a family of large fish with rich, oily, firm flesh. When purchasing tuna for preparations in which the fish is uncooked or only partially cooked, be sure to purchase from a reputable and reliable source or fishmonger; the tuna should be firm, have a translucent deep red color, and be free of any fishy aroma.

vinaigrette A vinaigrette is a simple mixture of oil and vinegar, plus seasonings. It is most often used as a dressing for salad but can also be used as a marinade or sauce for meat, poultry, or seafood

vinegars Each type of vinegar has a unique flavor profile and an acidic character that makes it particularly suited to certain salads and salad dressings.

balsamic A specialty of the Italian region of Emilia-Romagna, balsamic vinegar is an aged vinegar made from the unfermented grape juice, or must, of Trebbiano grapes. Aged in a series of wooden casks of decreasing sizes, each of a different wood, balsamic grows sweeter and more mellow with time.

champagne White wine vinegar made with Champagne grapes is lighter, milder, and sweeter than most white wine vinegars.

cider Made from apples, cider vinegar is noted for its distinctive apple flavor. For the best results, buy real apple cider vinegar, not cider-flavored distilled vinegar.

raspberry Flowery and sweet, this vinegar is made from white wine vinegar flavored and colored by the addition of raspberries.

red wine Sharply acidic, red wine vinegar is produced when red wine is fermented for a second time.

seasoned rice Popular in Asian cooking, rice vinegar is a clear, mild tasting, and slightly sweet vinegar produced from fermented glutinous rice. It is available plain or seasoned with sugar and salt; the latter is marketed as seasoned rice vinegar.

sherry True sherry vinegar from Spain, labeled "vinagre de Jerez," has a slightly sweet, nutty taste, a result of aging in oak.

white wine Light in flavor and pale in color, this vinegar can be produced from a variety of white wines, such as Chardonnay or Sauvignon Blanc.

watercress This member of the mustard family has round, deep-green leaves on delicate stems. Watercress has a refreshing, peppery flavor that turns bitter with age.

index

OXMOOR HOUSE

Oxmoor House books are distributed by Sunset Books
80 Willow Road, Menlo Park, CA 94025
Telephone: 650 324 1532
VP and Associate Publisher **Jim Childs**
Director of Marketing **Sydney Webber**
Oxmoor House and Sunset Books are divisions
of Southern Progress Corporation

WILLIAMS-SONOMA, INC.

Founder & Vice-Chairman **Chuck Williams**

WILLIAMS-SONOMA NEW FLAVORS SERIES

Conceived and produced by Weldon Owen Inc.
415 Jackson Street, Suite 200, San Francisco, CA 94111
Telephone: 415 291 0100 Fax: 415 291 8841
www.weldonowen.com

In Collaboration with Williams-Sonoma, Inc.
3250 Van Ness Avenue, San Francisco, CA 94109

A WELDON OWEN PRODUCTION
Copyright © 2009 Weldon Owen Inc. and Williams-Sonoma, Inc.

All rights reserved, including the right of reproduction
in whole or in part in any form.

First printed in 2009
Printed in Singapore

Printed by Tien Wah Press
10 9 8 7 6 5 4 3 2 1
Library of Congress Cataloging-in-Publication Data is available.

ISBN-13: 978-0-8487-3272-1
ISBN-10: 0-8487-3272-3

WELDON OWEN INC.

Executive Chairman, Weldon Owen Group **John Owen**
CEO and President, Weldon Owen Inc. **Terry Newell**
Senior VP, International Sales **Stuart Laurence**
VP, Sales and New Business Development **Amy Kaneko**
Director of Finance **Mark Perrigo**

VP and Publisher **Hannah Rahill**
Executive Editor **Jennifer Newens**
Senior Editor **Dawn Yanagihara**

VP and Creative Director **Gaye Allen**
Art Director **Kara Church**
Senior Designer **Ashley Martinez**
Designer **Stephanie Tang**
Photo Manager **Meghan Hildebrand**

Production Director **Chris Hemesath**
Production Manager **Michelle Duggan**
Color Manager **Teri Bell**

Photographer **Kate Sears**
Food Stylist **Karen Shinto**
Prop Stylist **Danielle Fisher**

Additional Photography Getty Images: Frank Rothe, page 14–15; Dan
Goldberg: Pages 18, 119; Tucker + Hossler: pages 23, 25, 29, 38, 45, 62, 65,
69, 77, 82, 98, 103, 109, 120, 125, 129, 134, 149; Jupiter Images: Tara Sgroi,
pages 27, 84; Photodisc: pages 52–53; Shutterstock: Cheryl A. Meyer, page
59; agefotostock: 78–79; IStockphoto: John Sigler, pages 110–111; Jupiter
Images: Victoria Pearson, page 117.

ACKNOWLEDGMENTS
Weldon Owen wishes to thank the following individuals for their kind
assistance: Photo Assistants **Victoria Wall** and **Sam Willard**; Food Stylist
Assistants **Fanny Pan** and **Alexis Machado**; Copy editor **Sharon Silva**;
Proofreader **Leslie Evans**; Indexer **Elizabeth Parson**.